Card's Creative **DESIGNER** Coloring Book

ALLEN M **CARD**

authorHOUSE®

AuthorHouse™
1663 Liberty Drive
Bloomington, IN 47403
www.authorhouse.com
Phone: 1 (800) 839-8640

Published by AuthorHouse 01/23/2019

ISBN: 978-1-5462-7753-8 (sc)
ISBN: 978-1-5462-7760-6 (e)

Print information available on the last page.

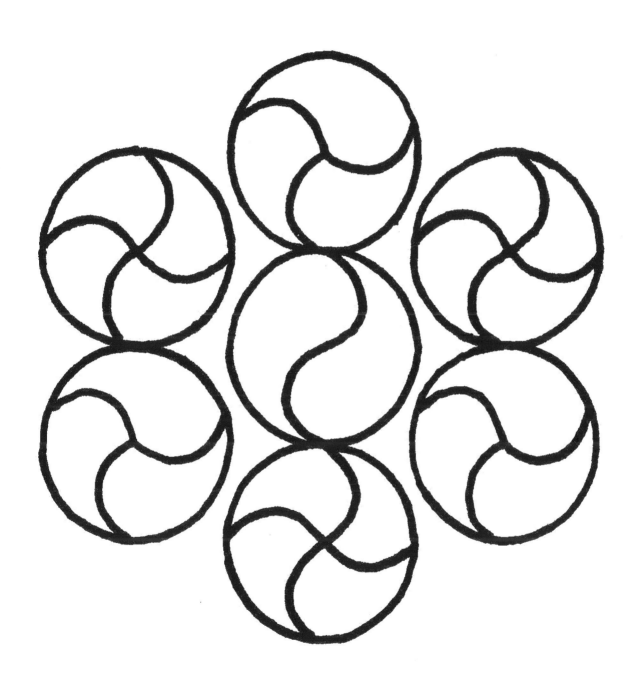

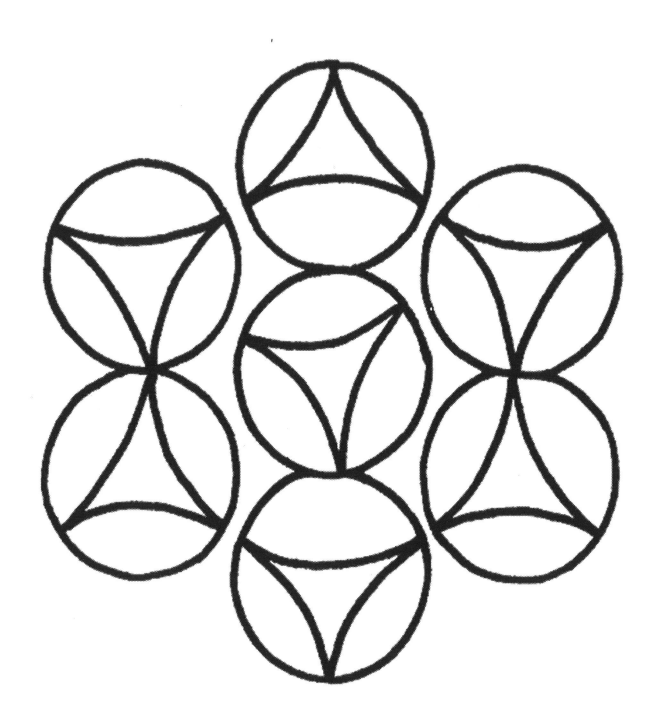

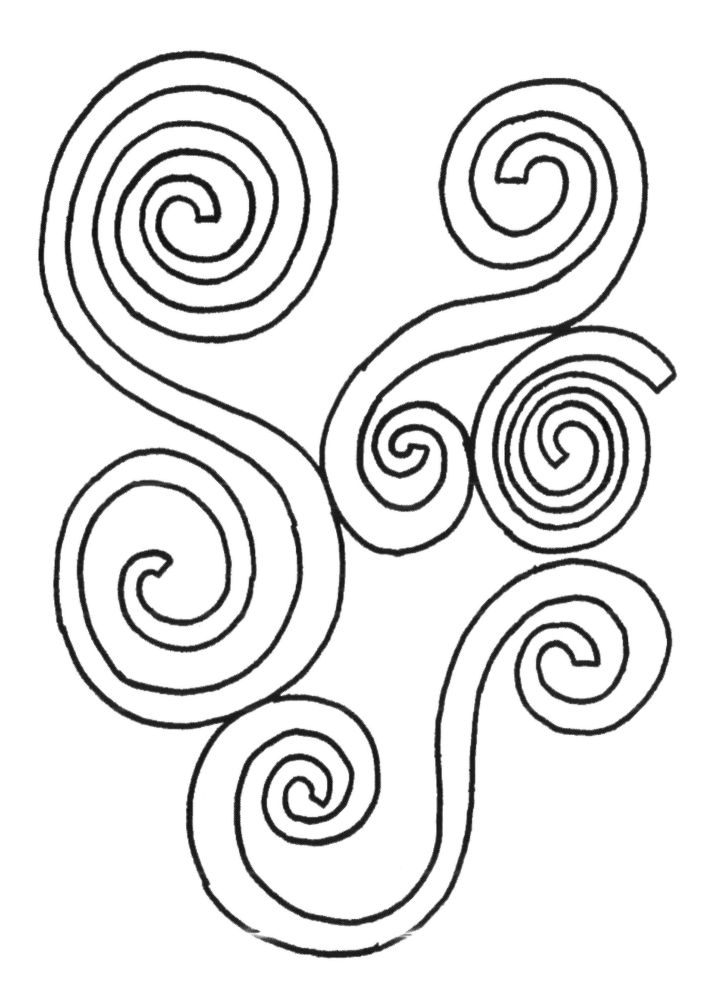

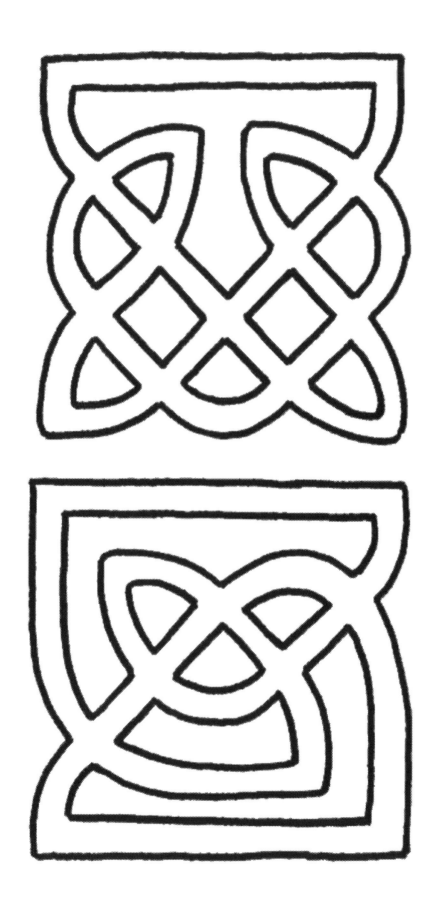

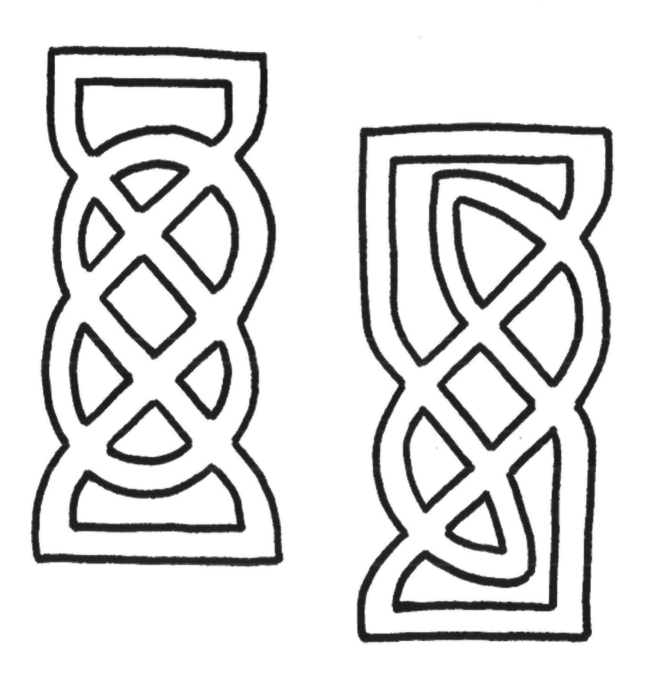

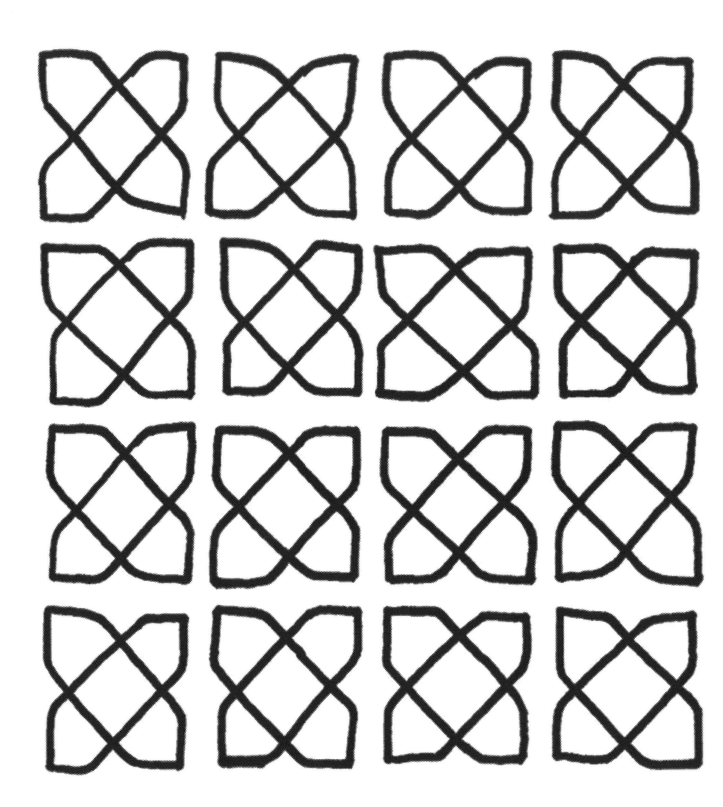

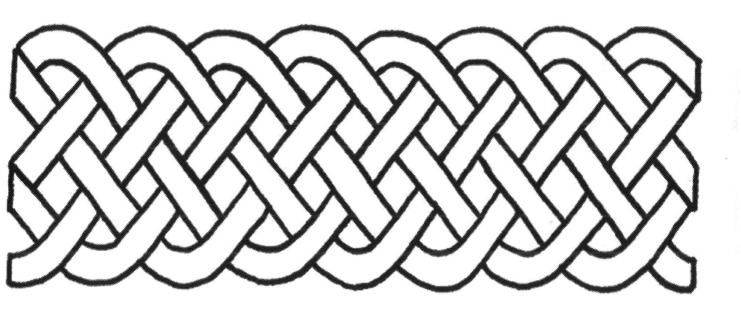

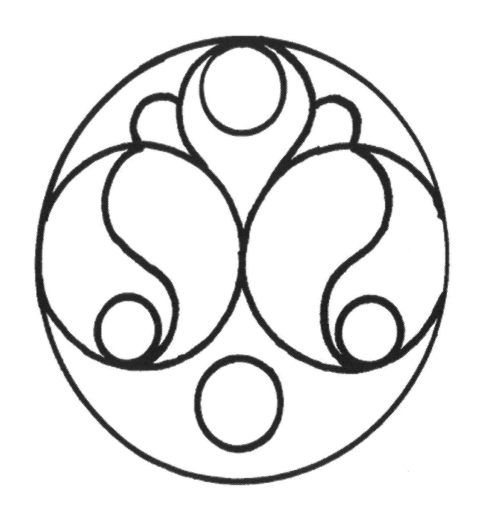

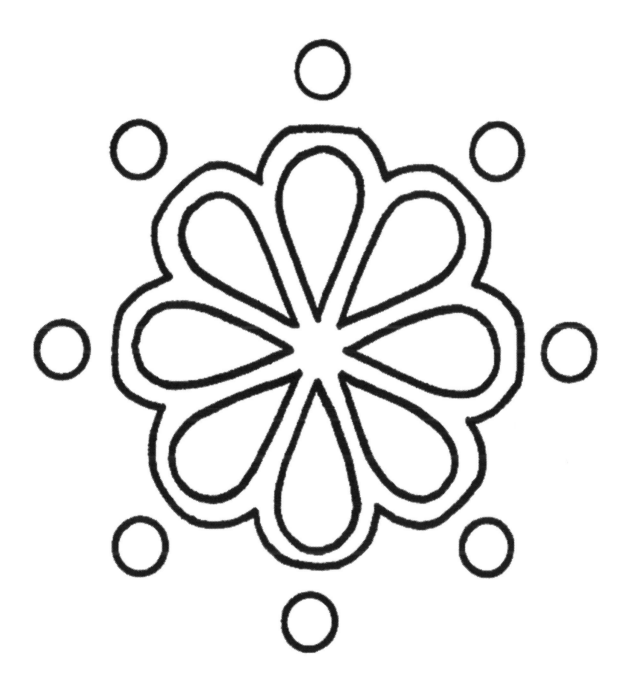

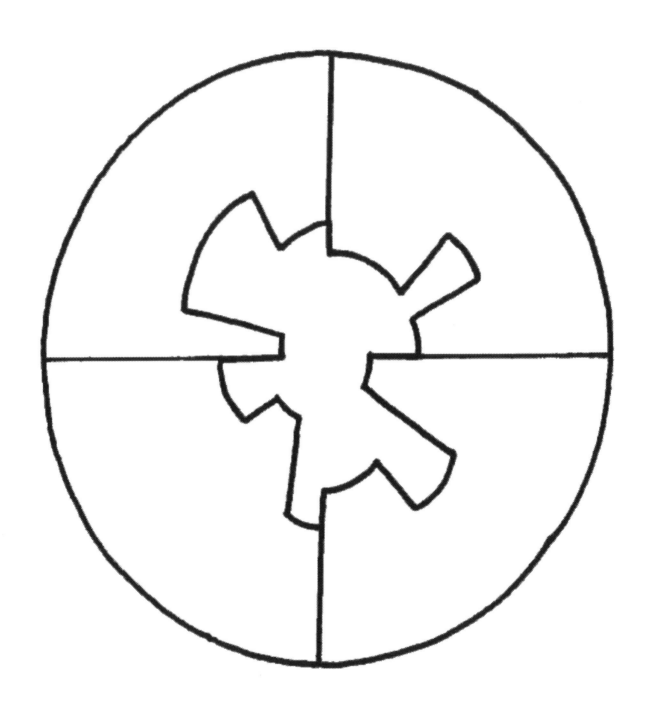

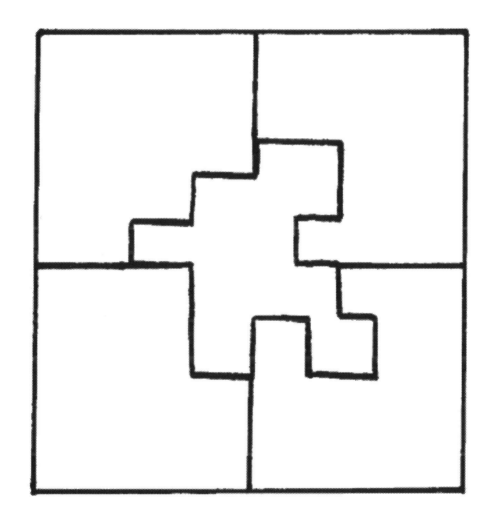

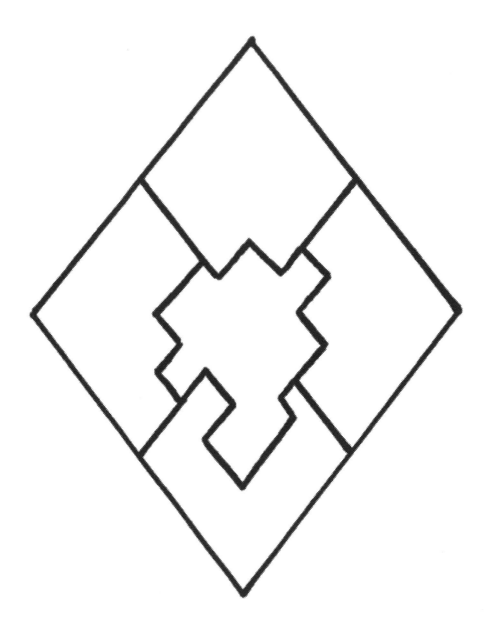

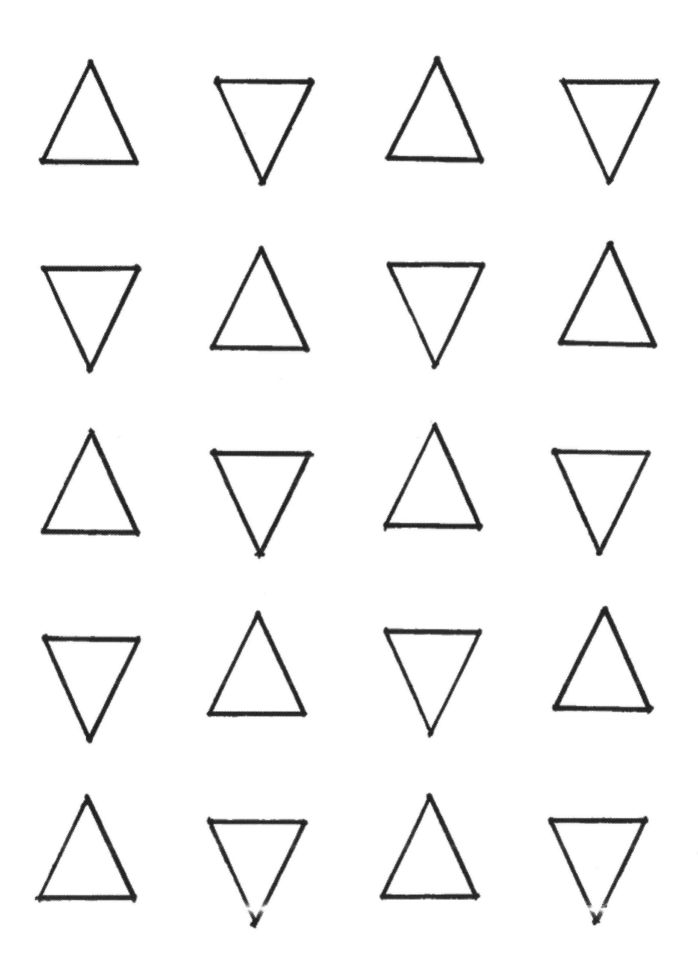

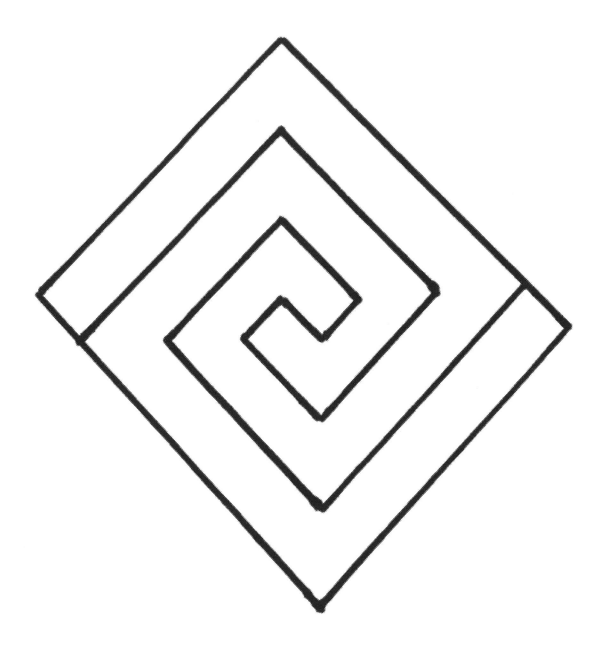

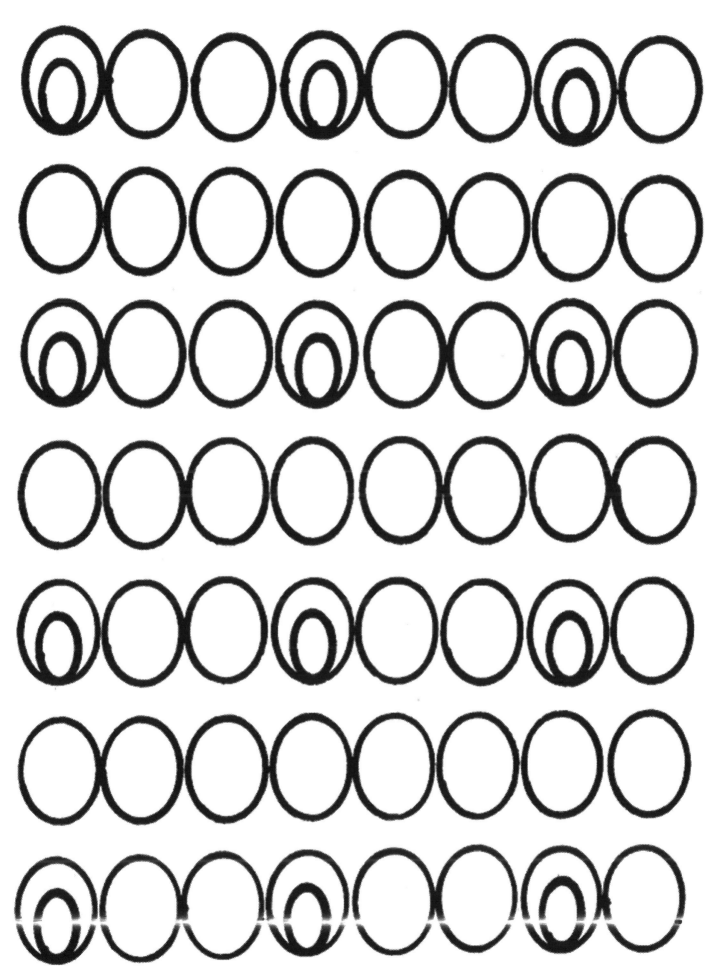

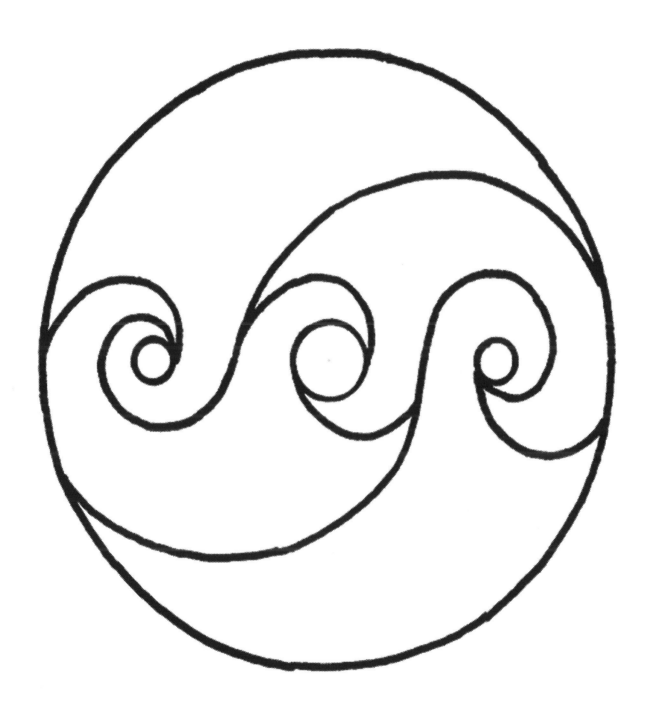

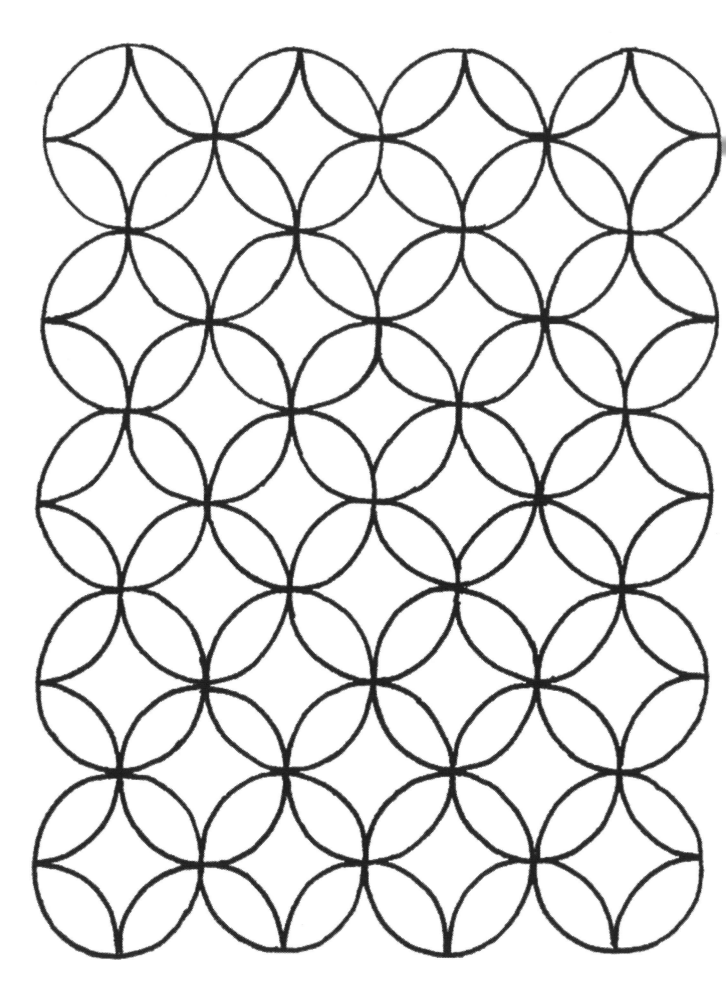

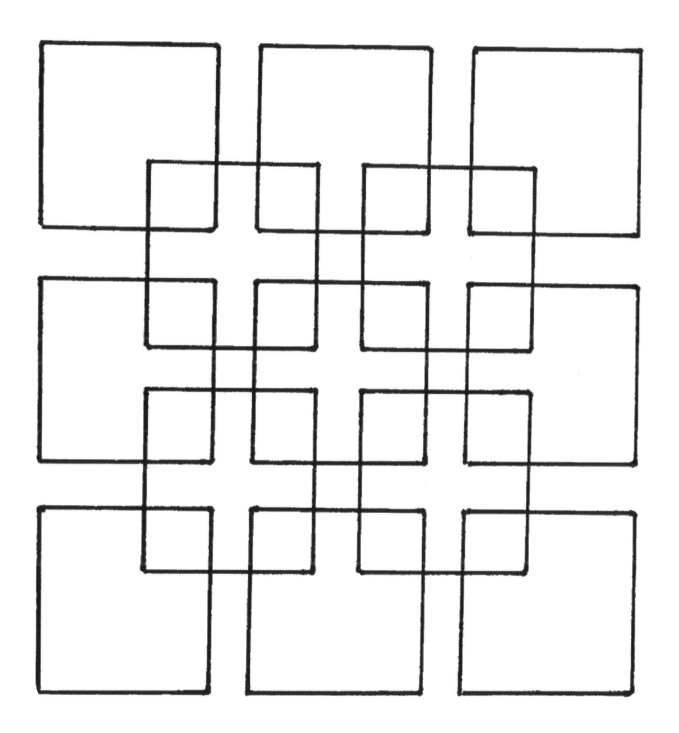

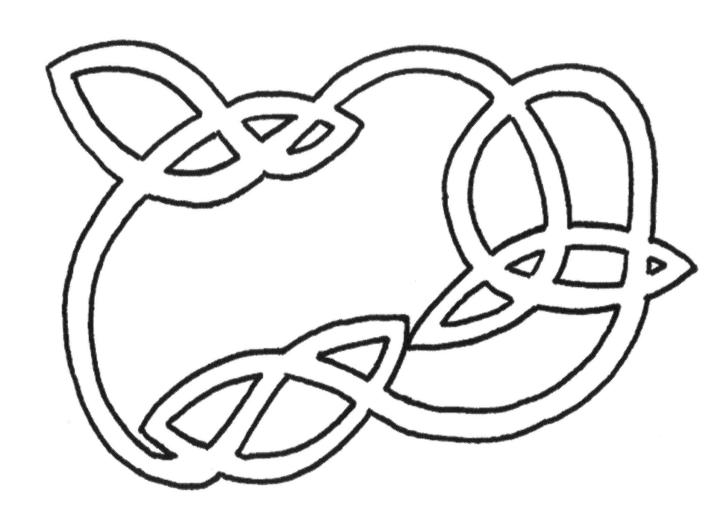

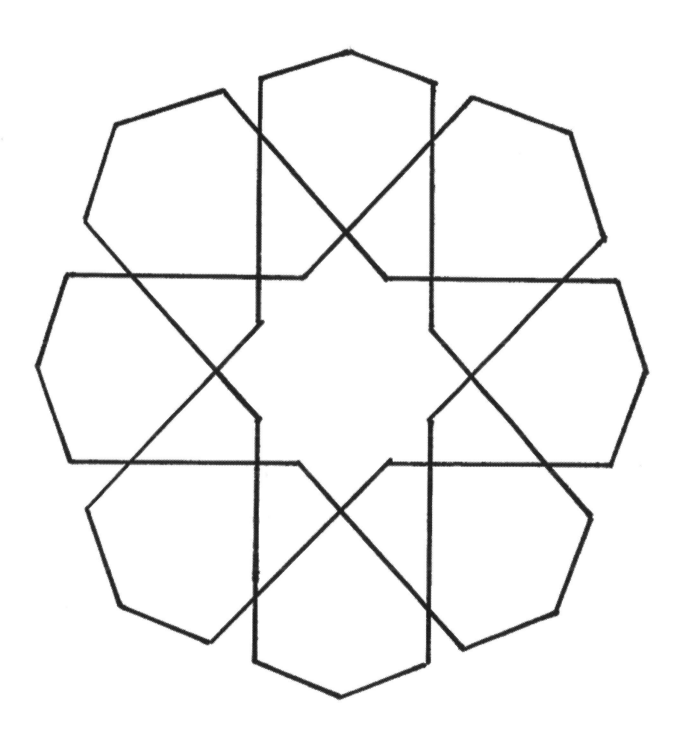

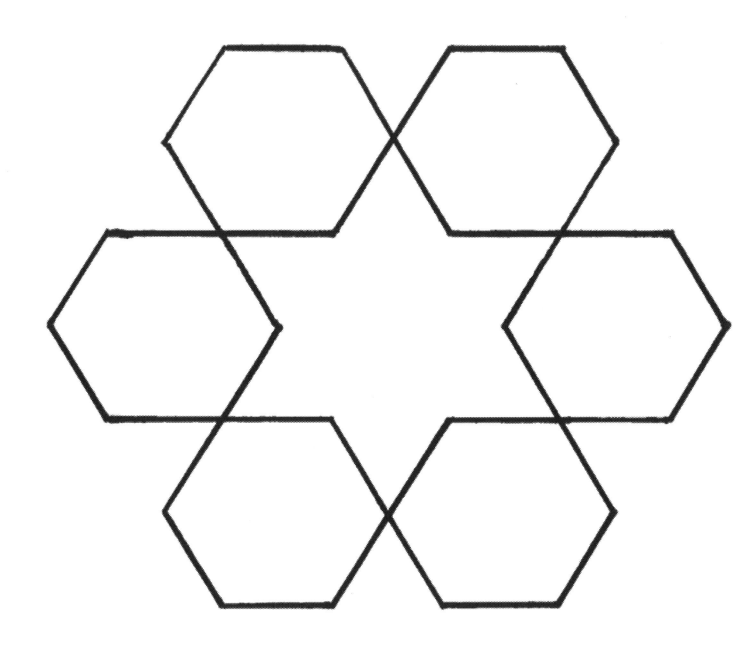

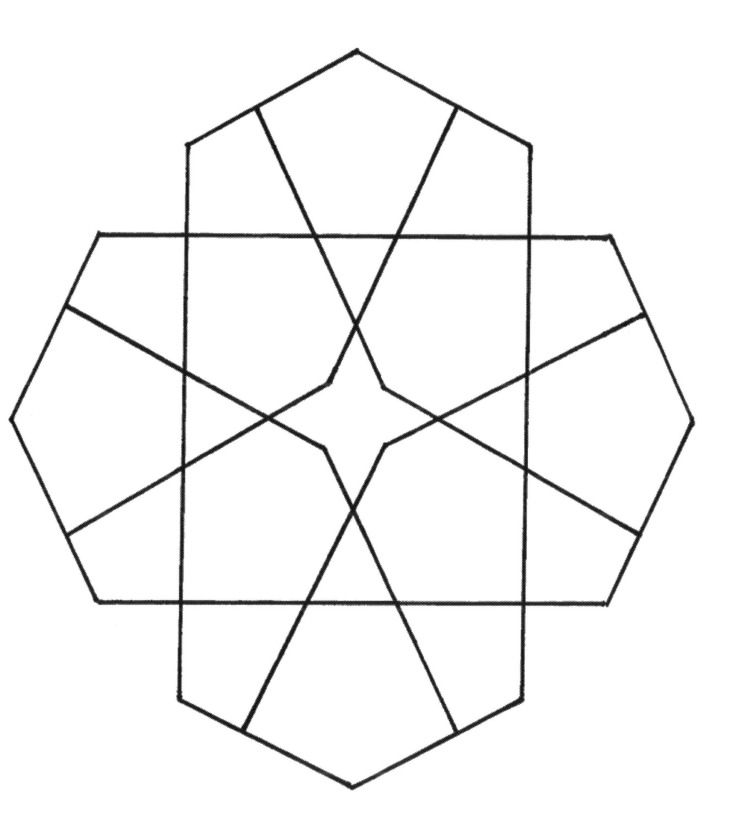

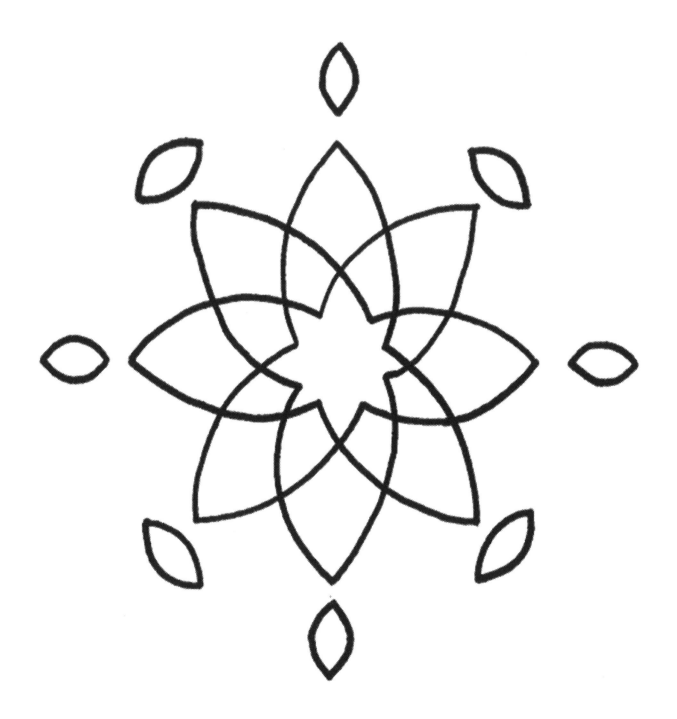

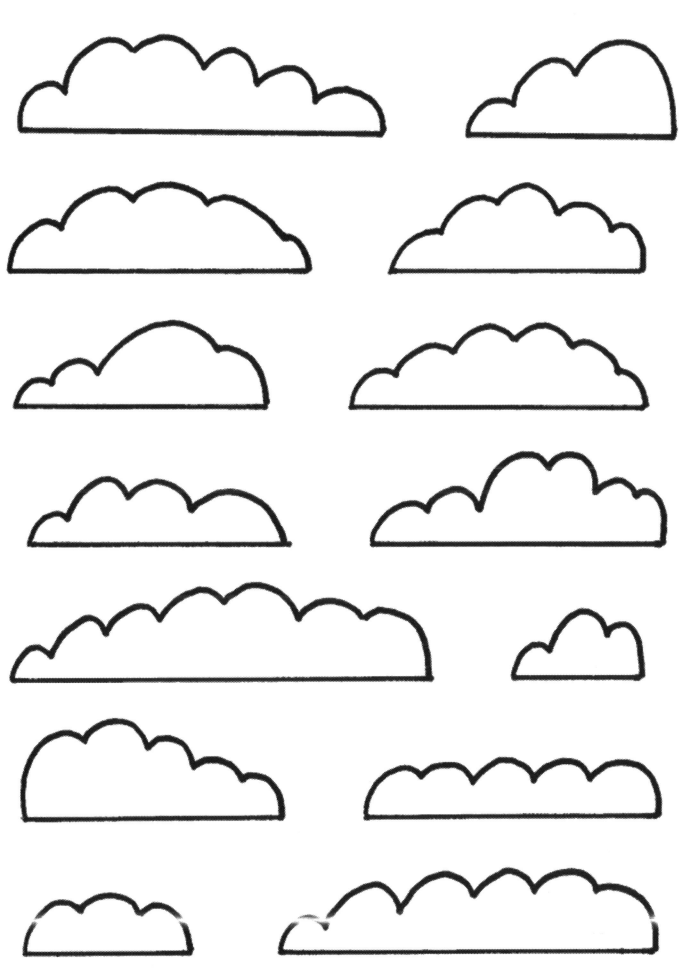

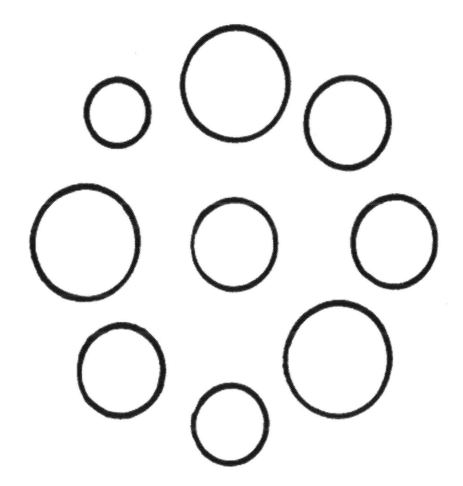

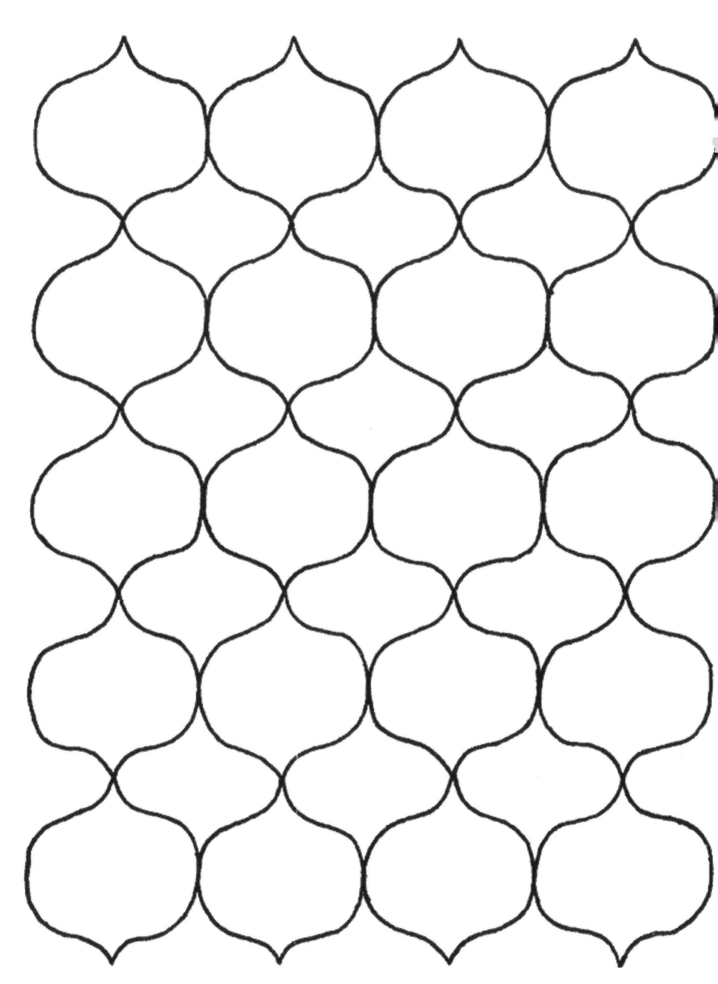

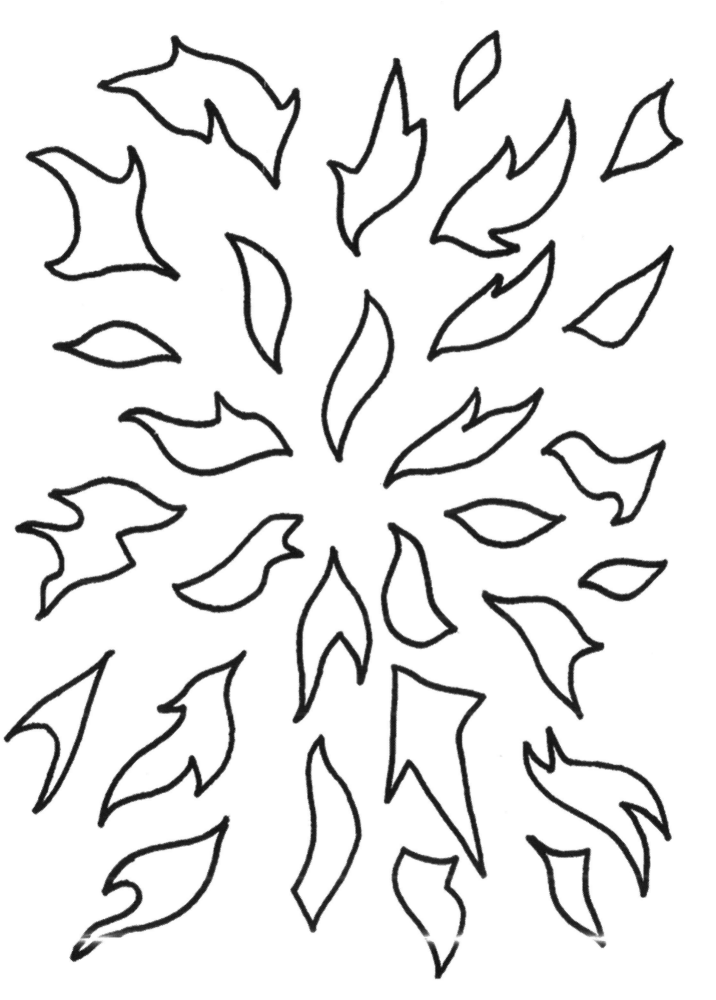

29

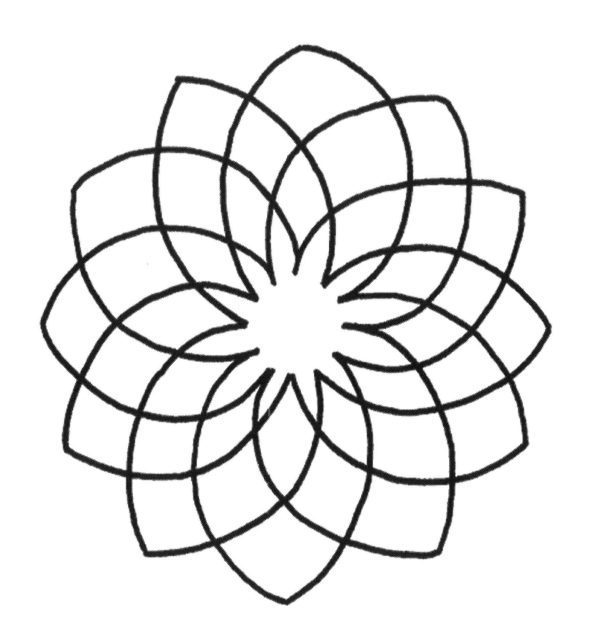

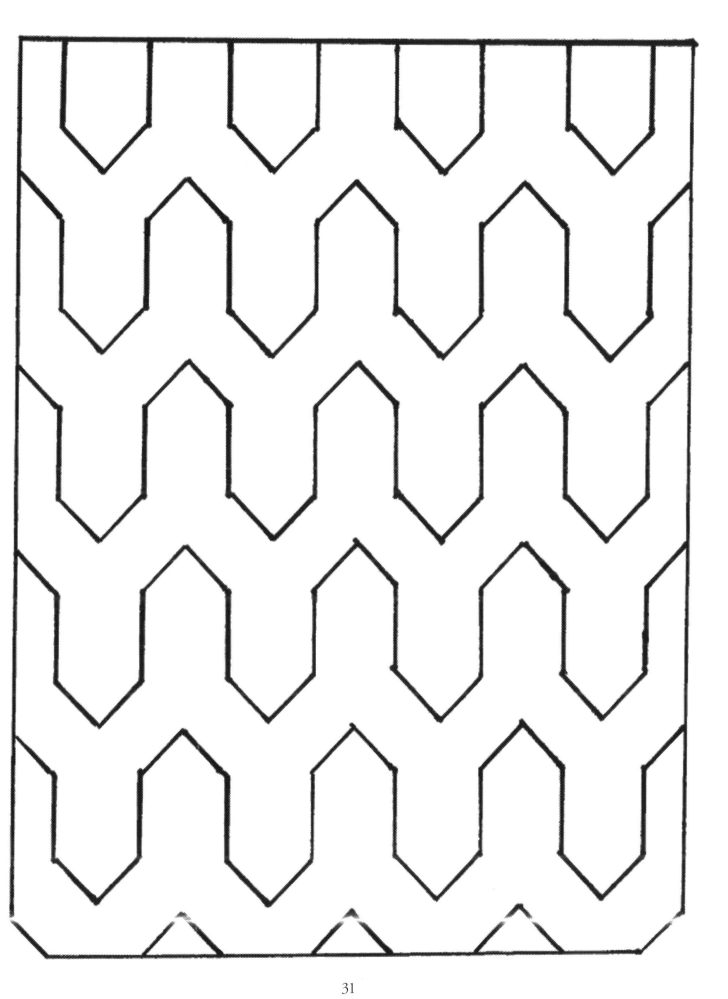

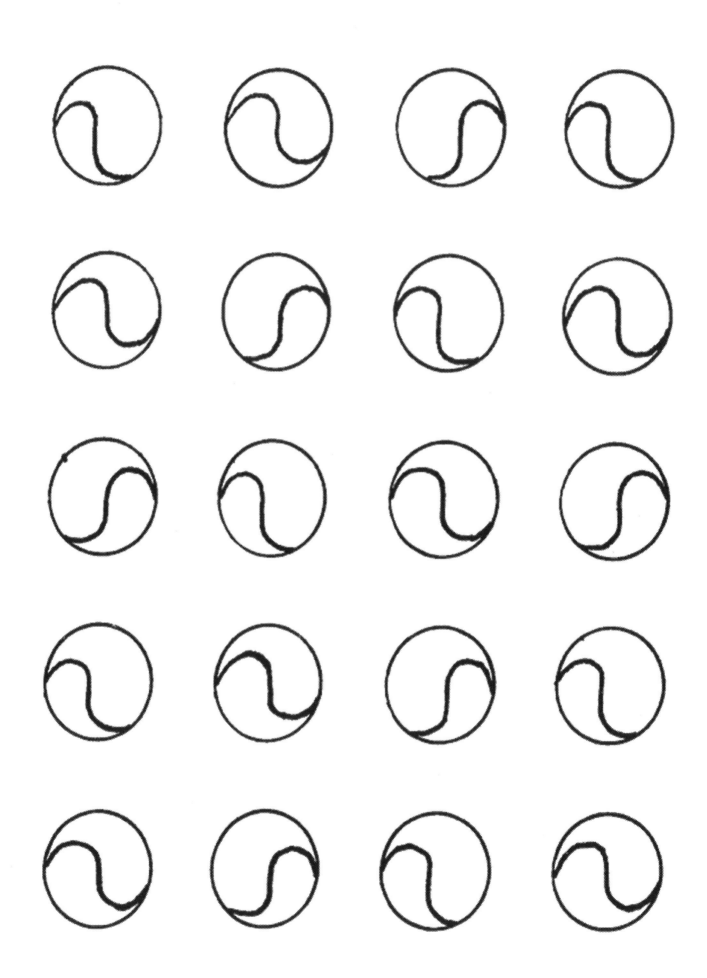

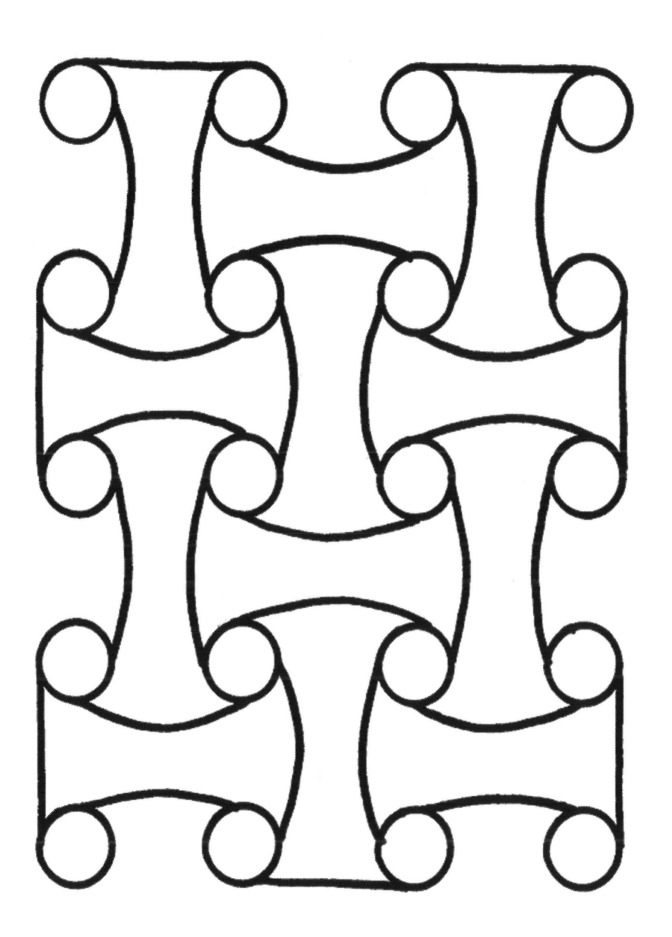

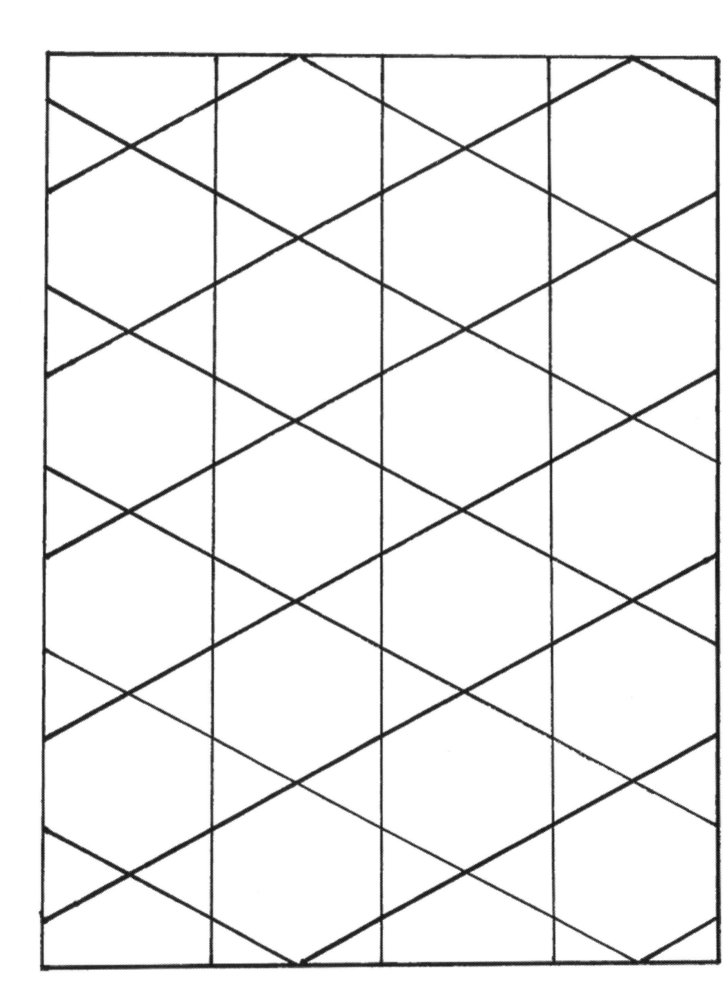

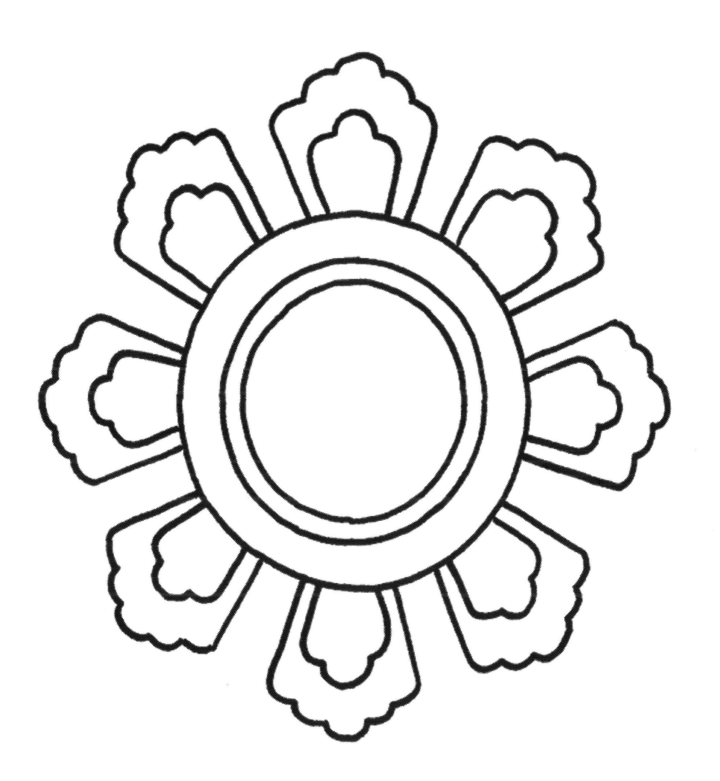

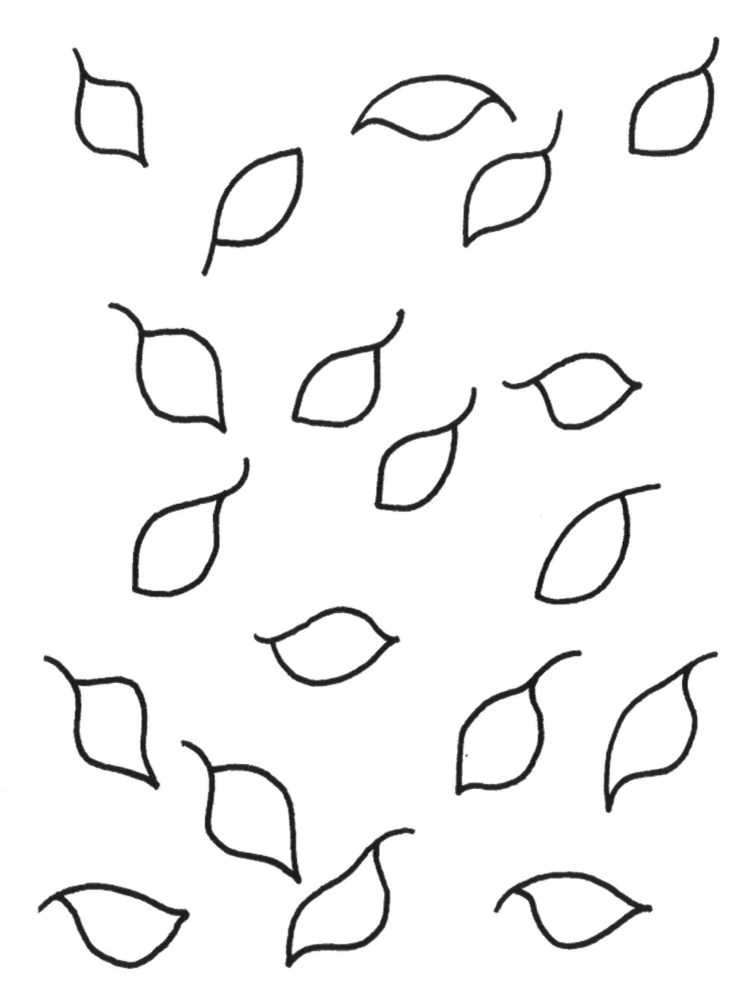

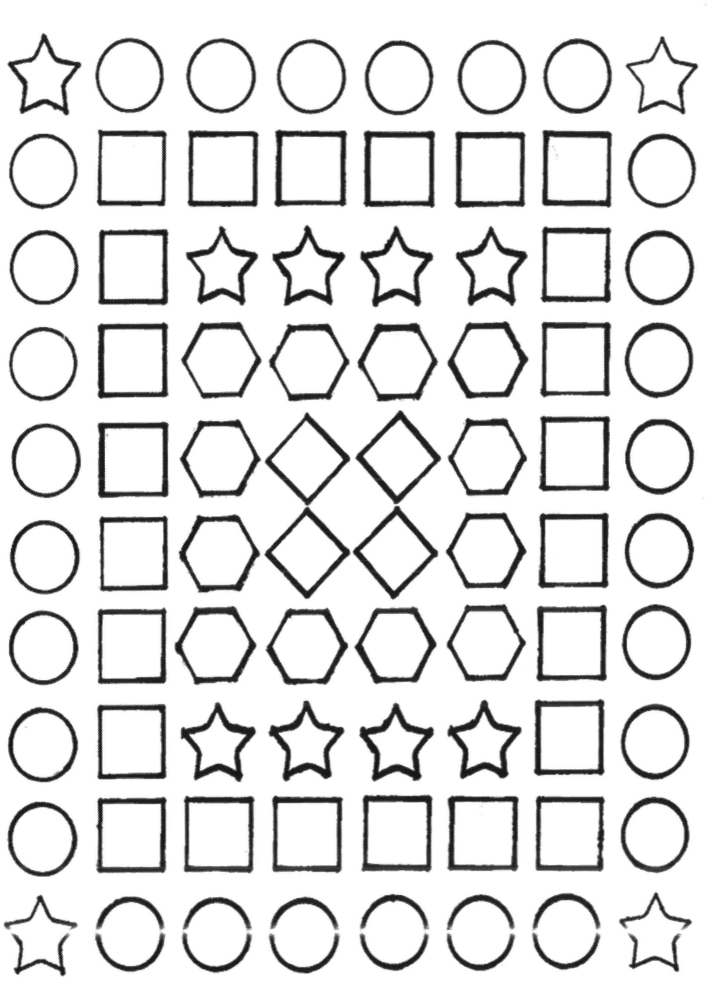

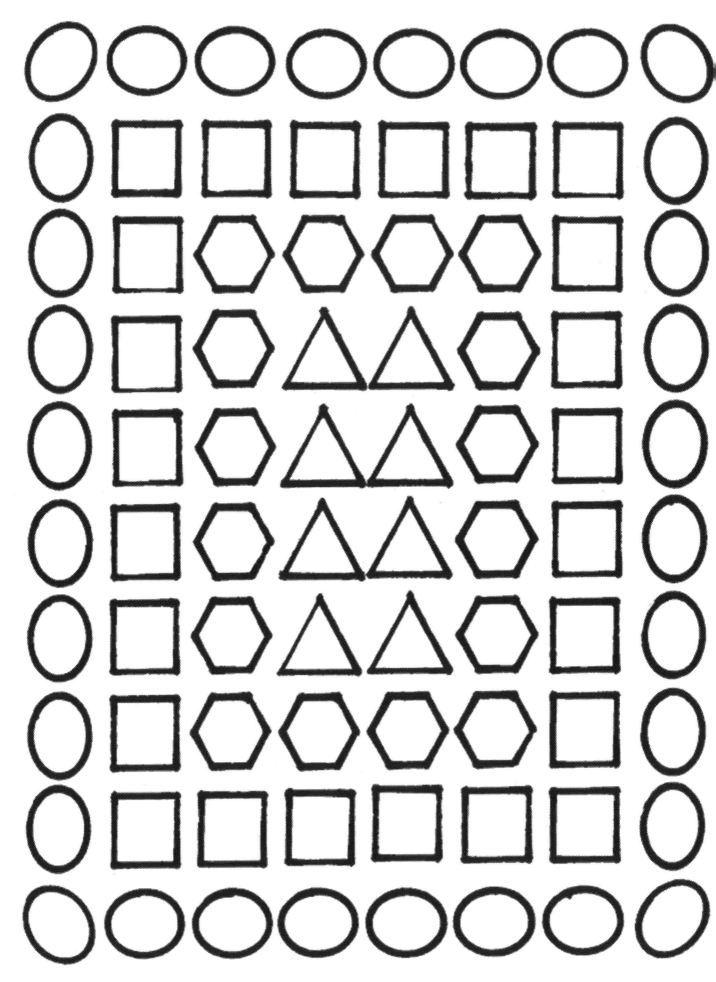

38

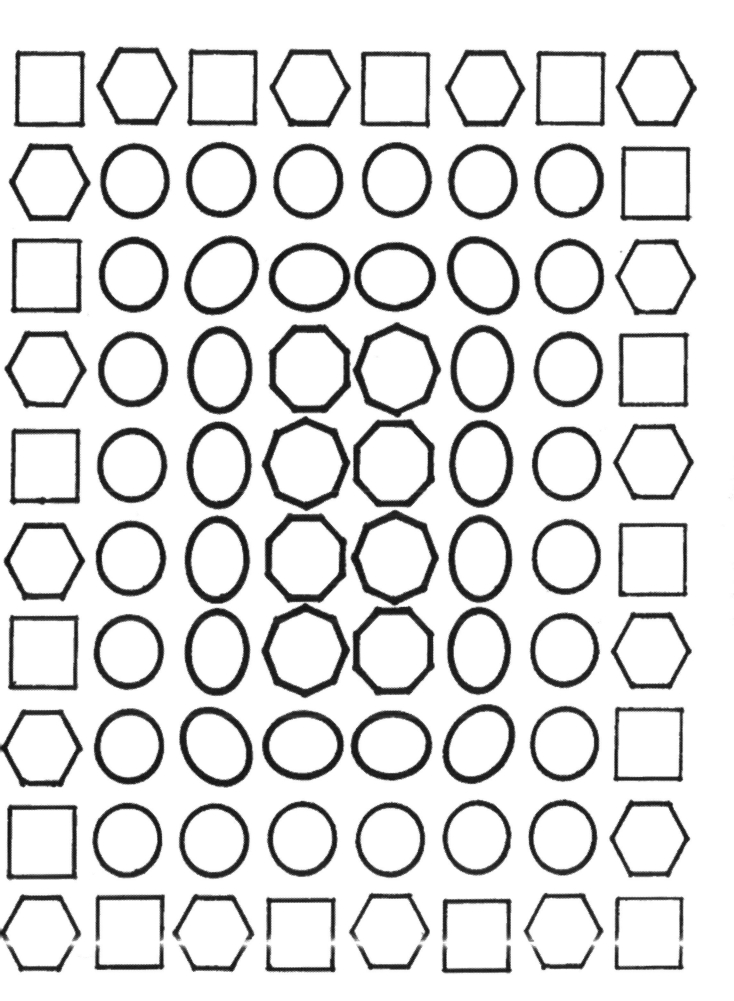

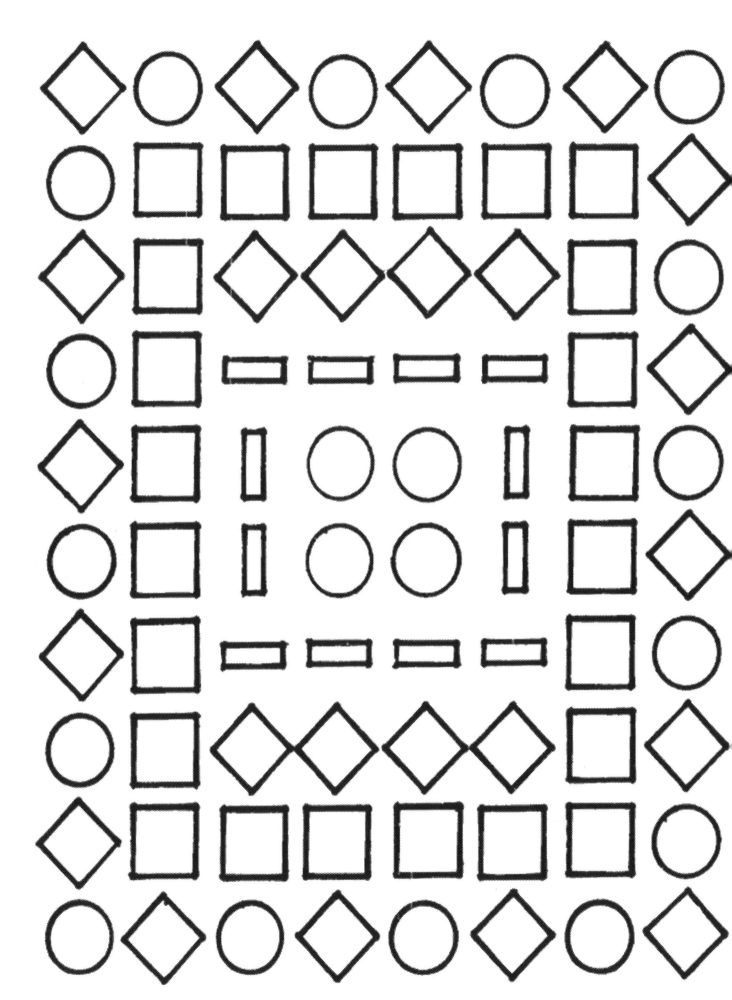

40

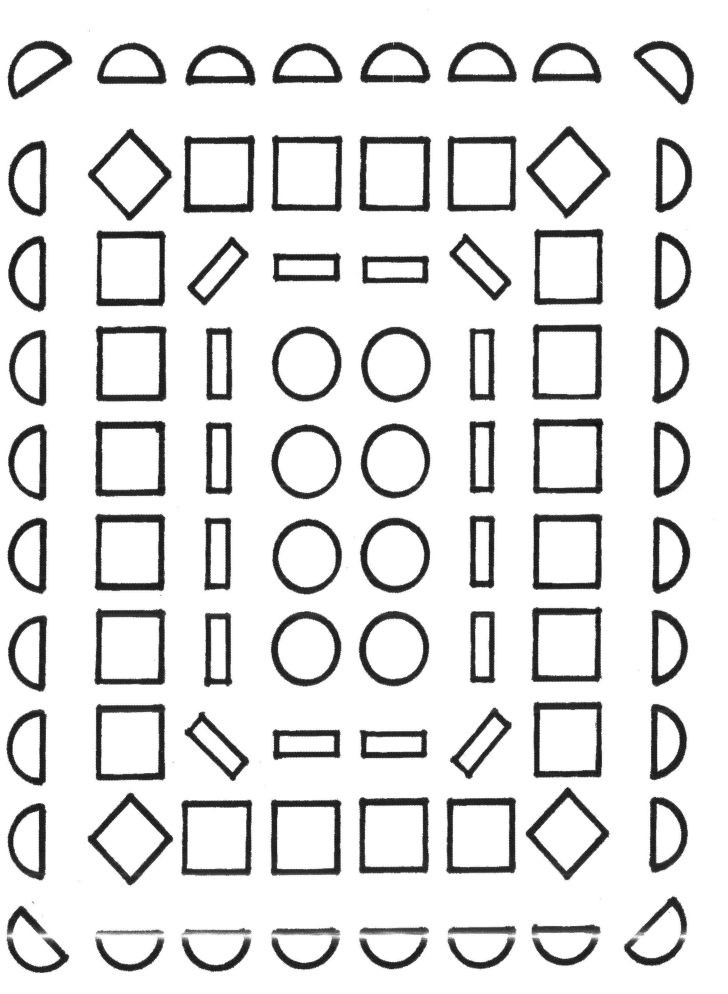

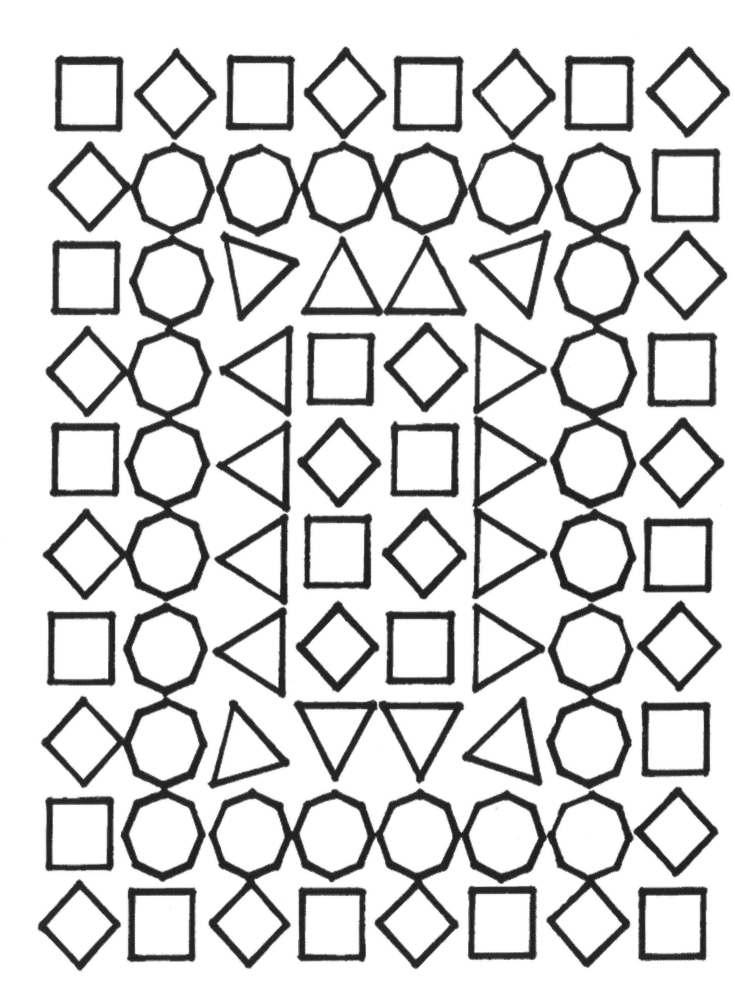

42

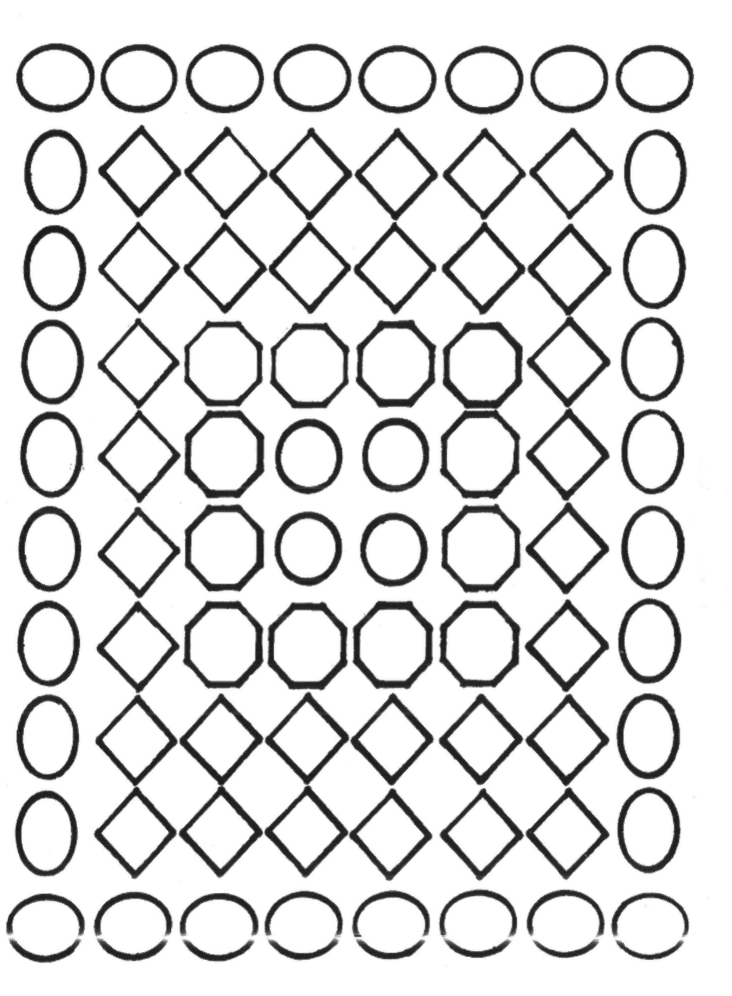

43

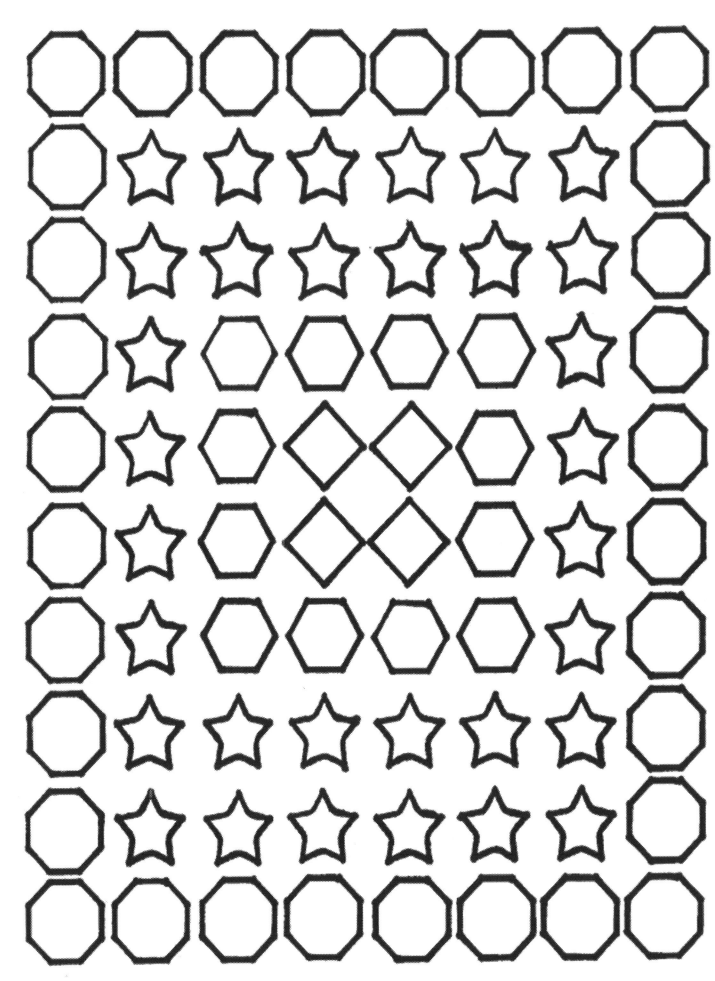

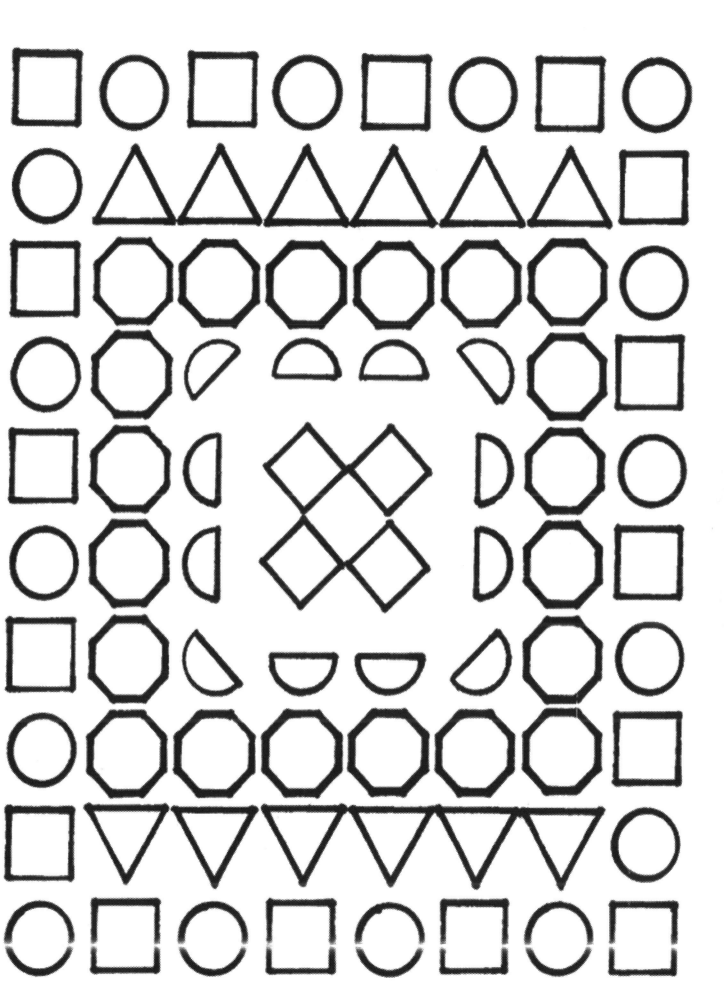

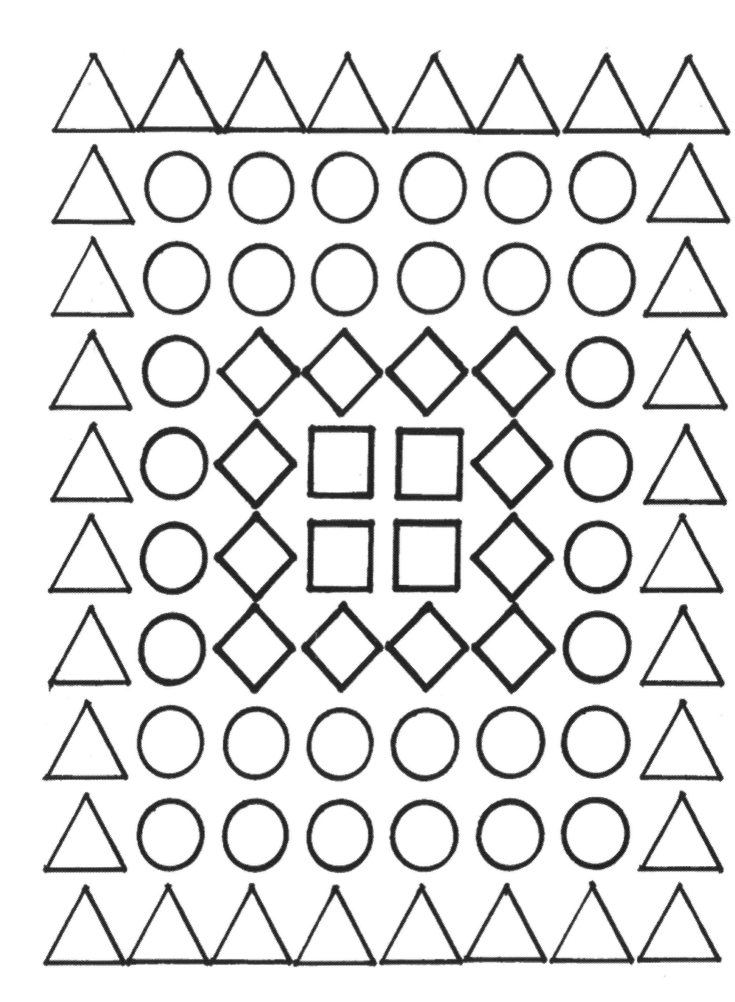

46

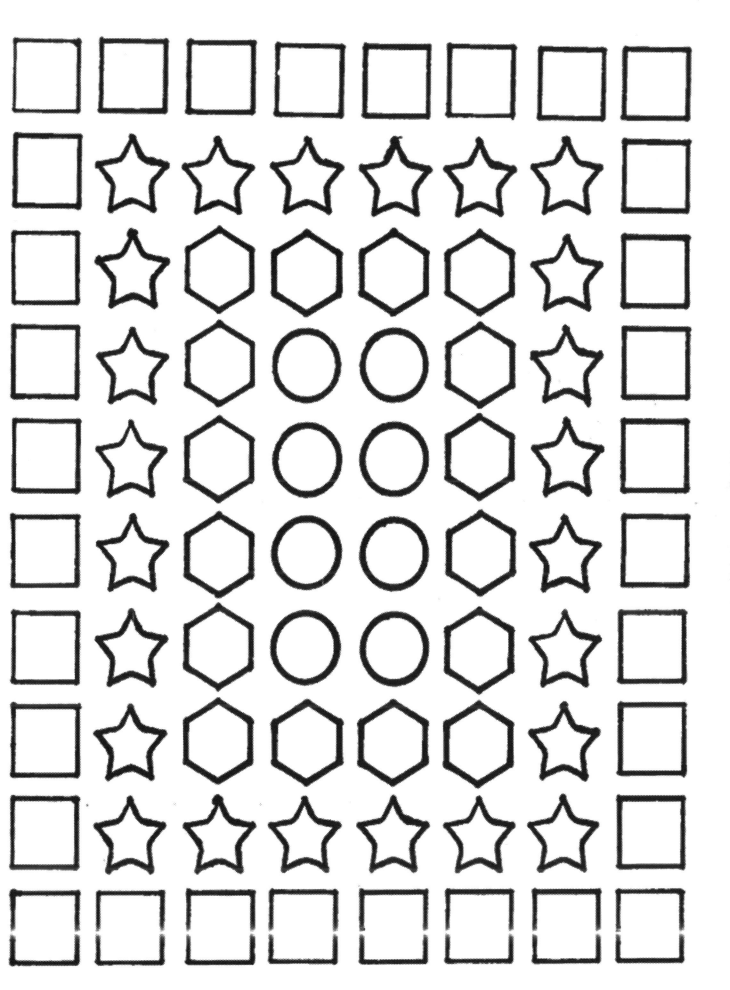

47

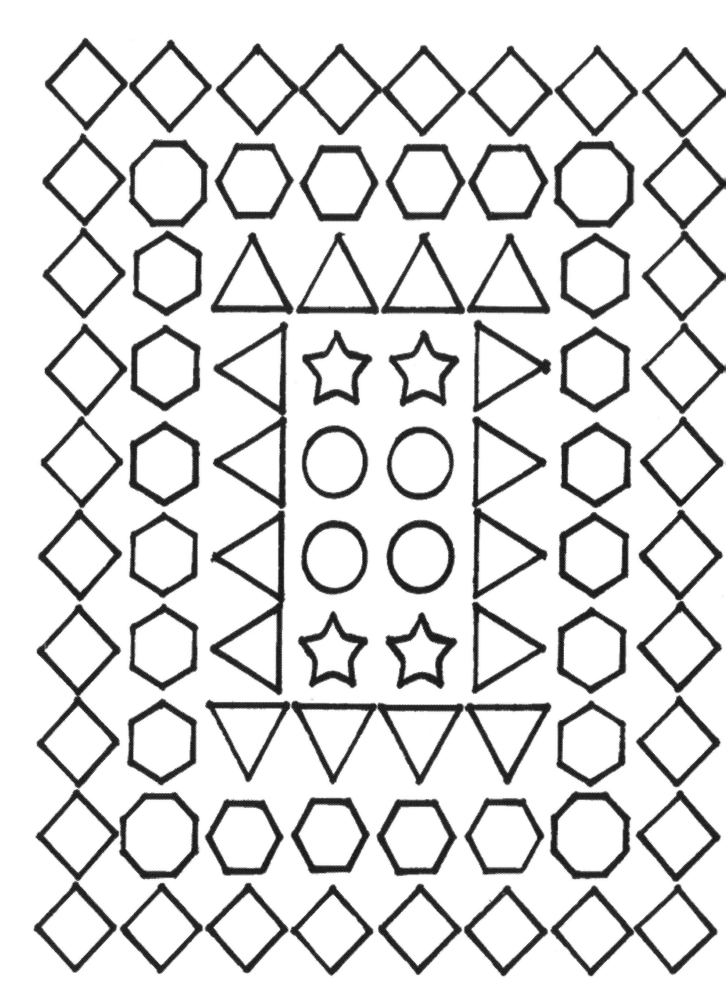

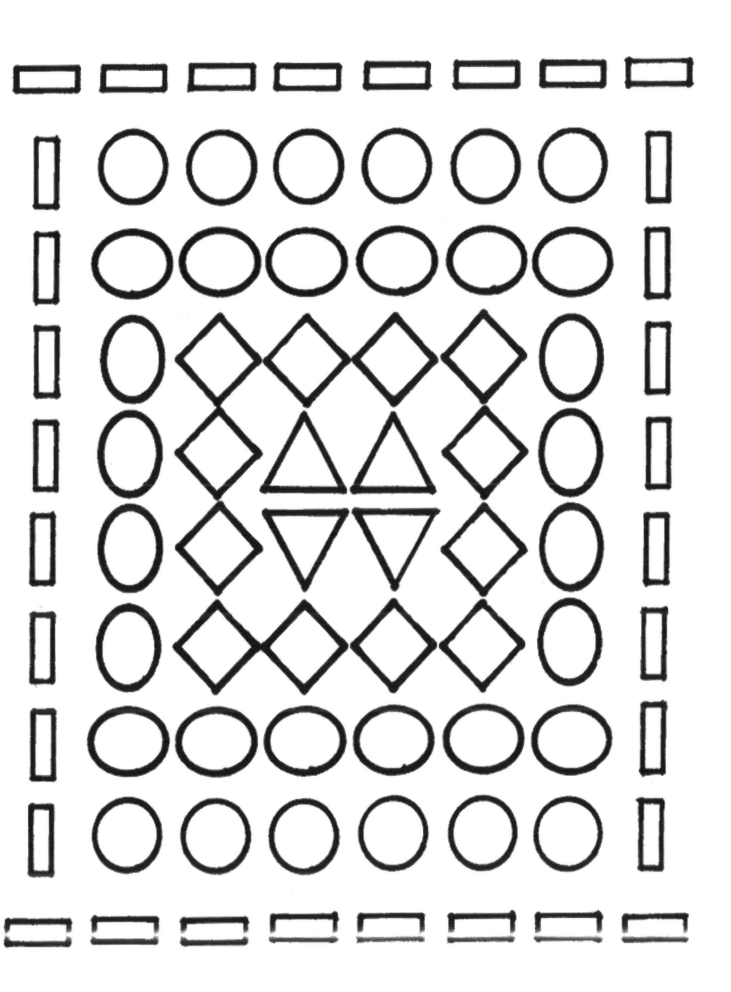

49

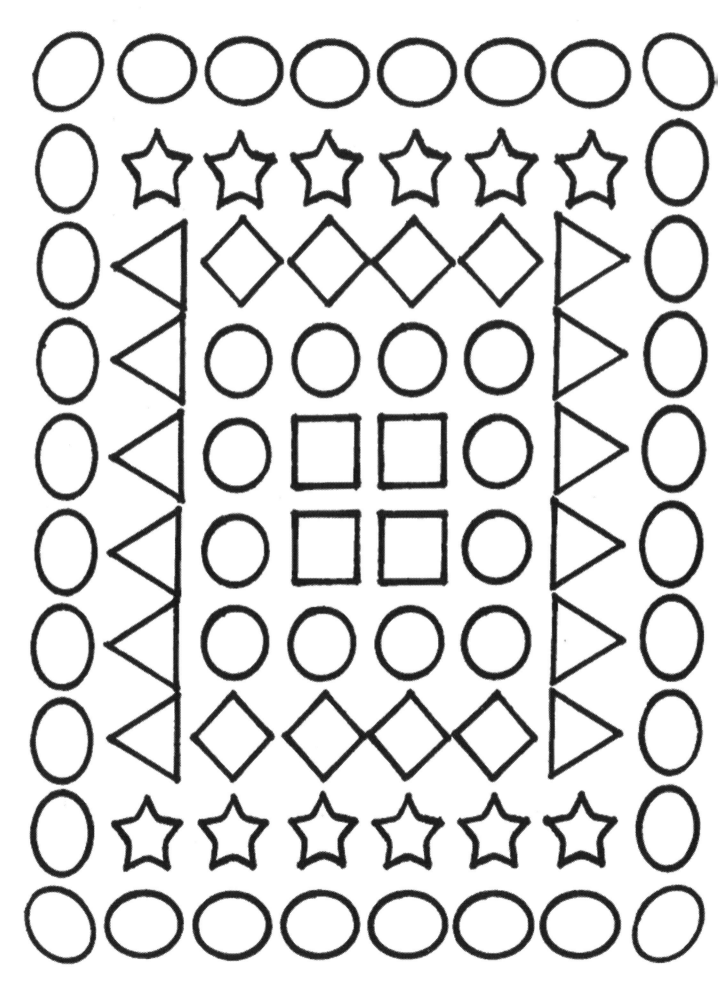

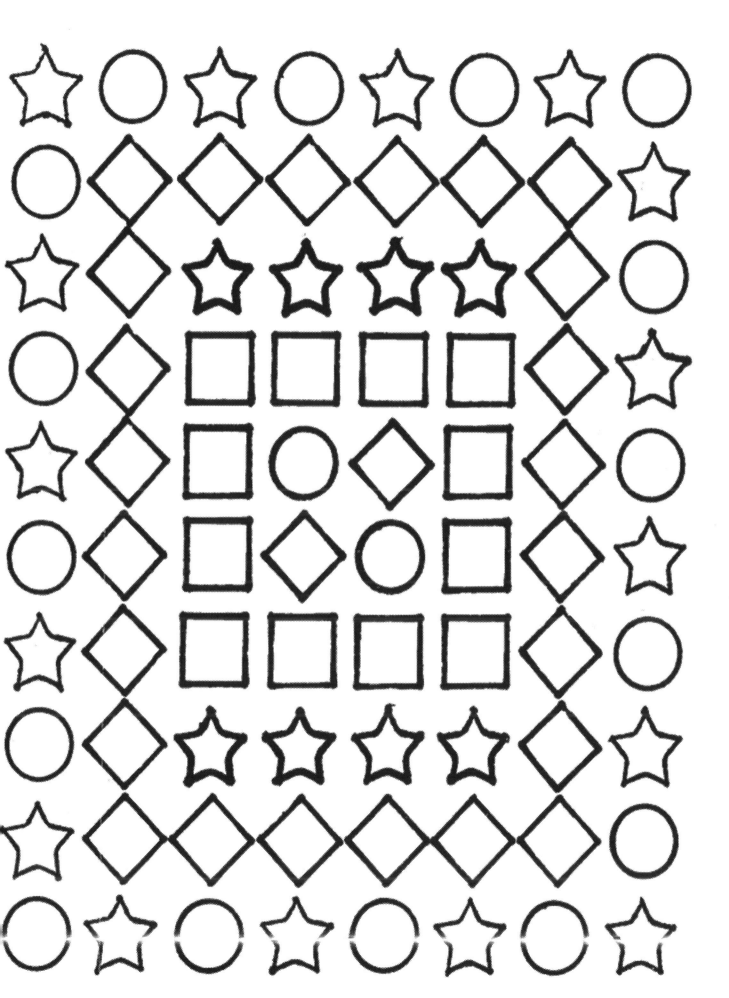

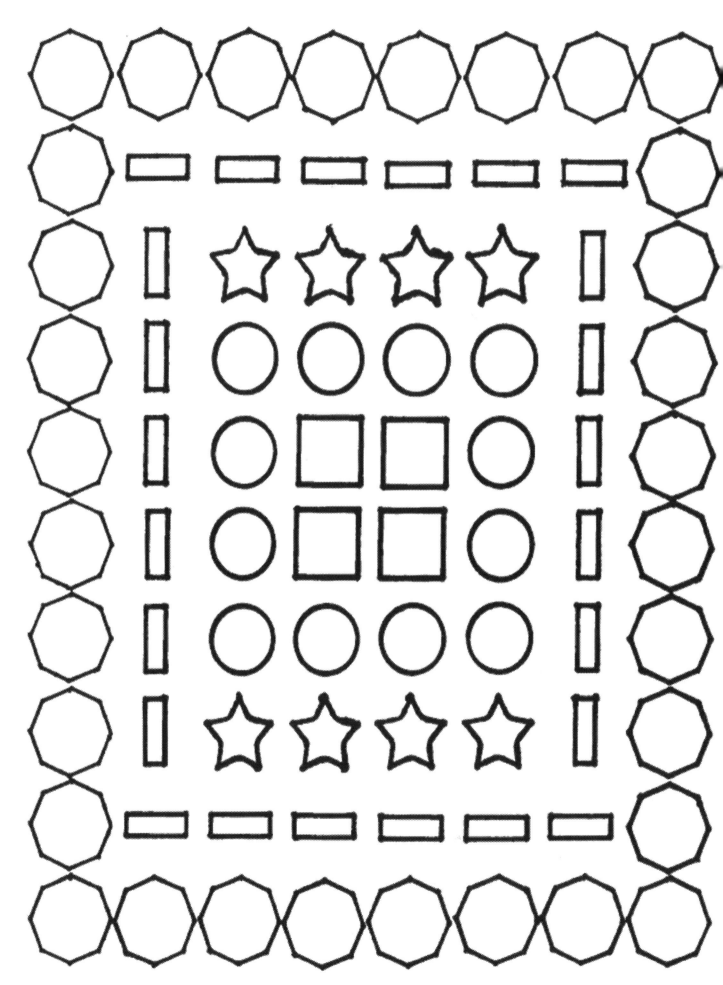

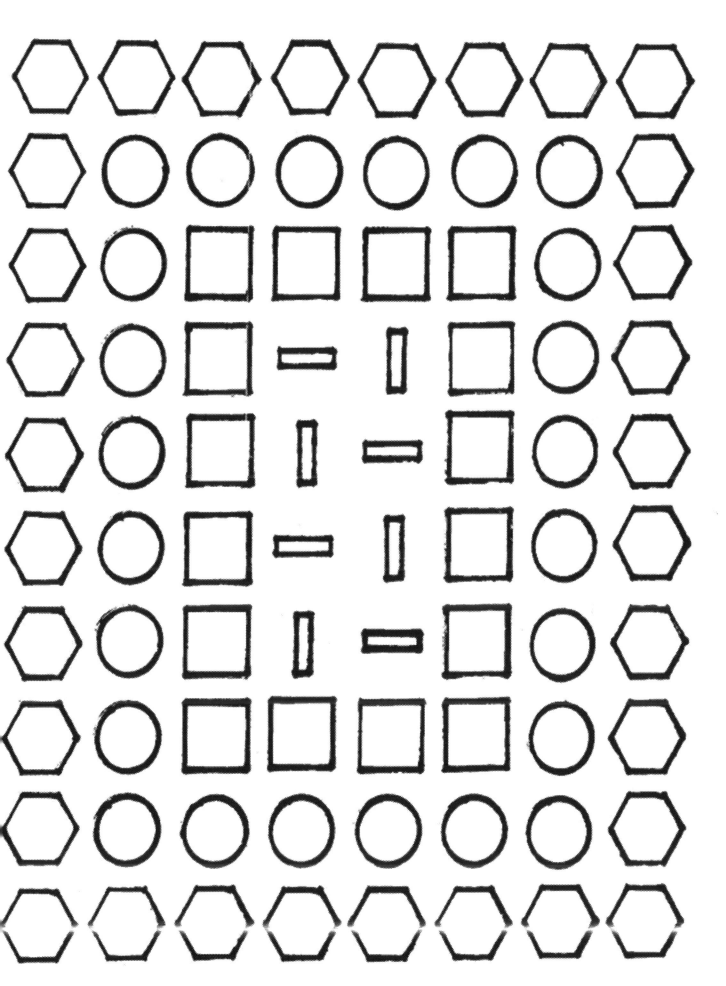

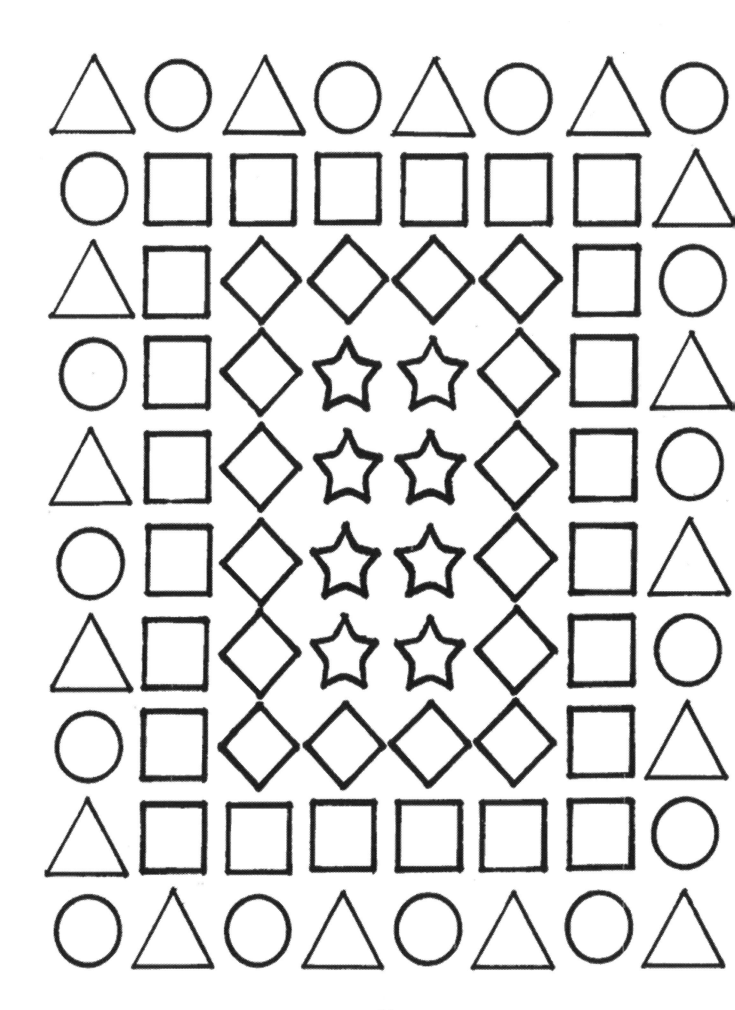

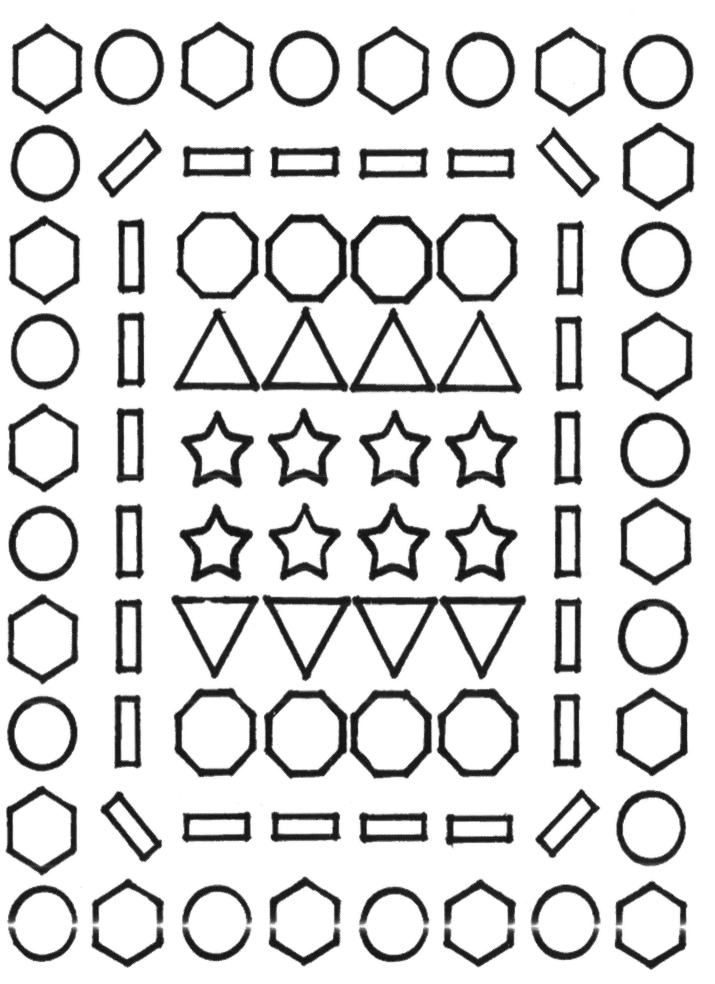

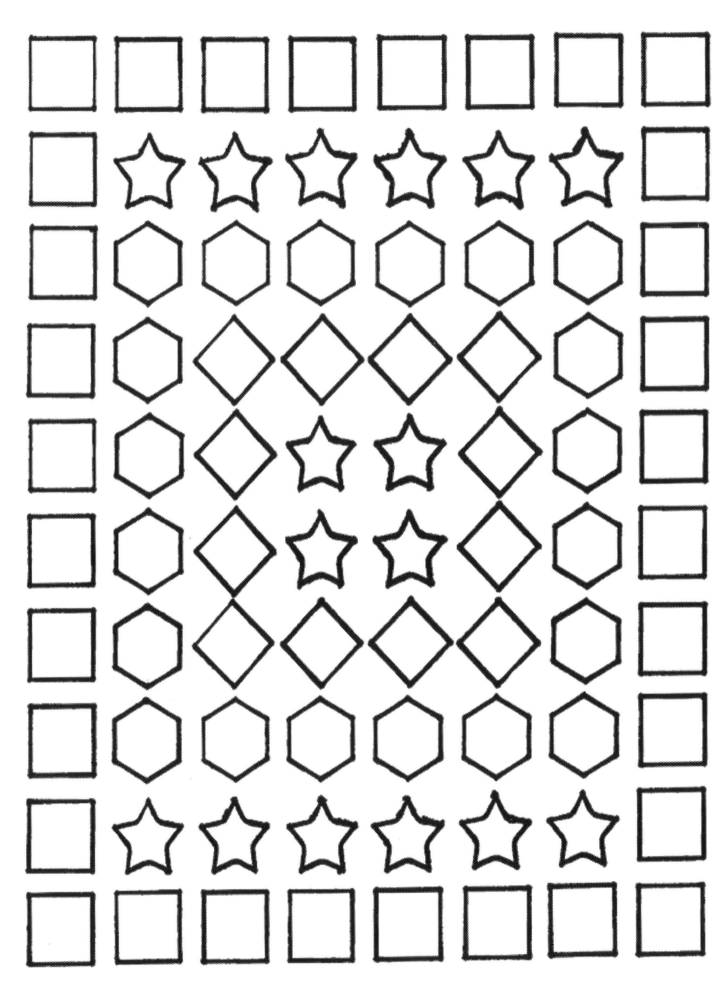

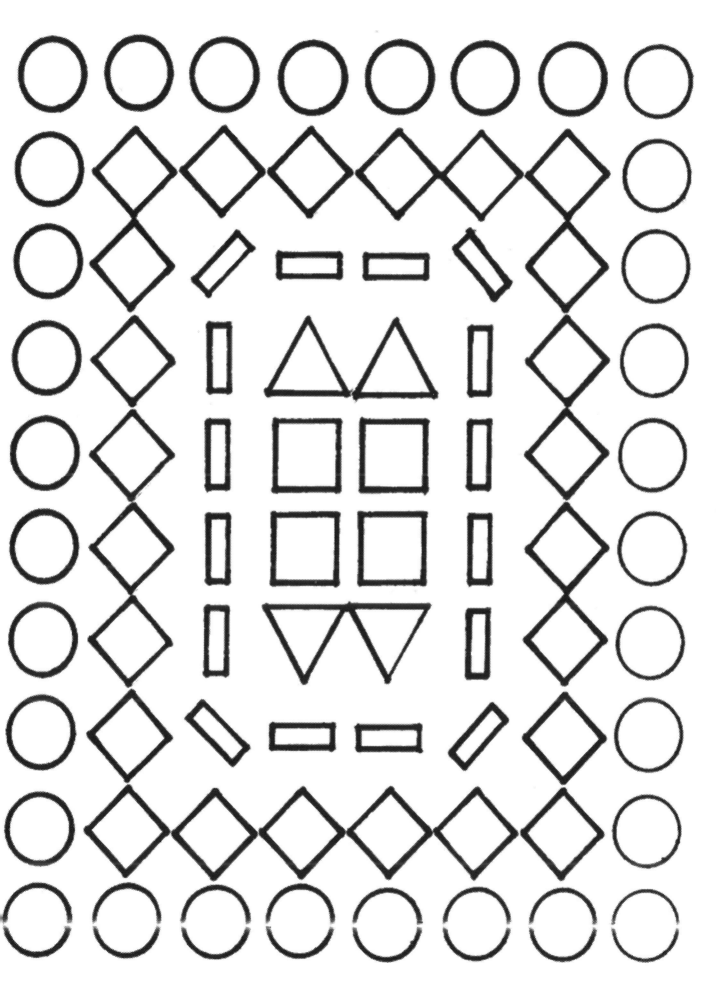

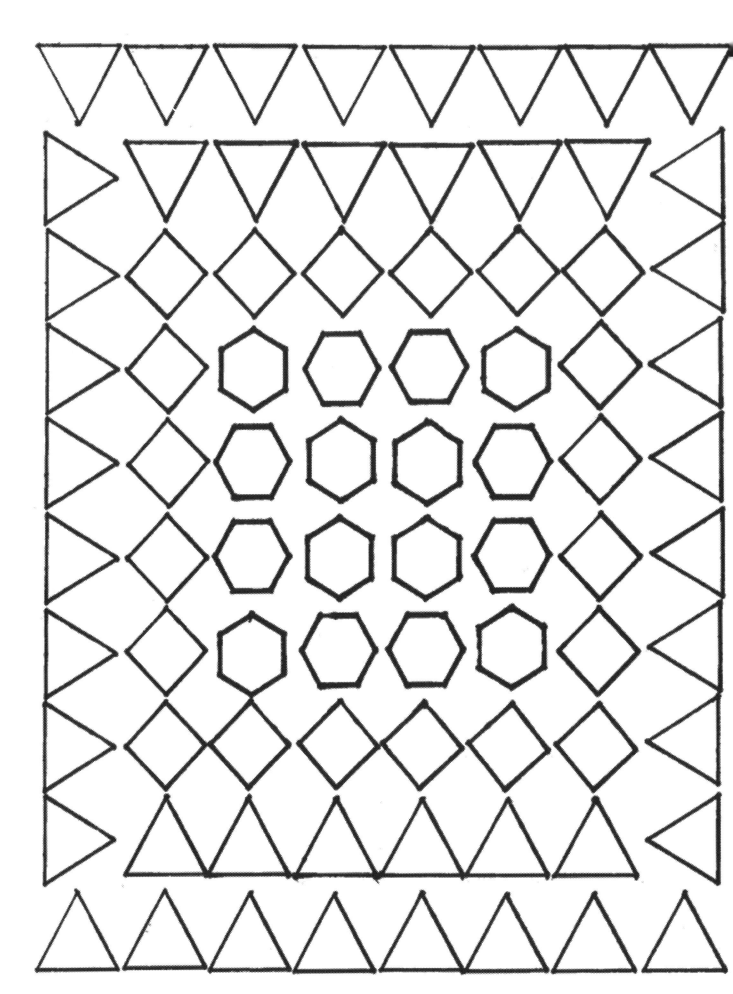

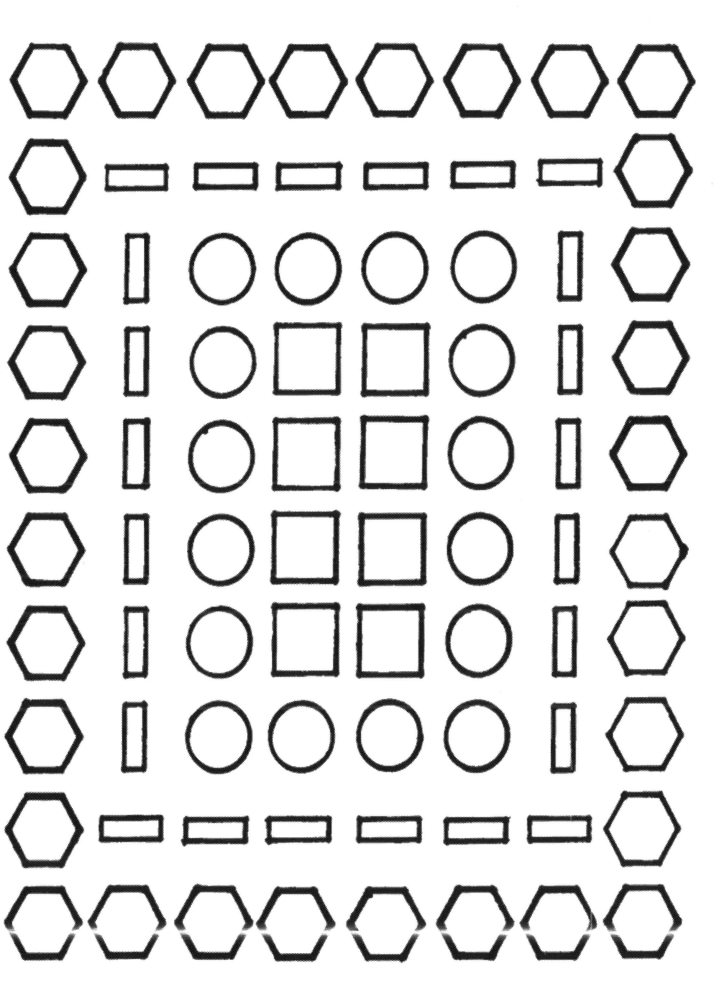

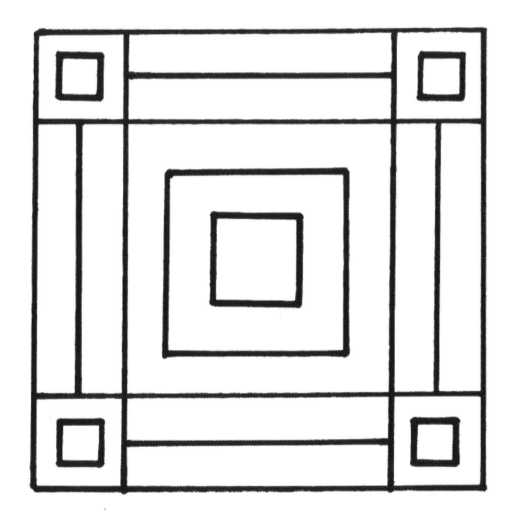

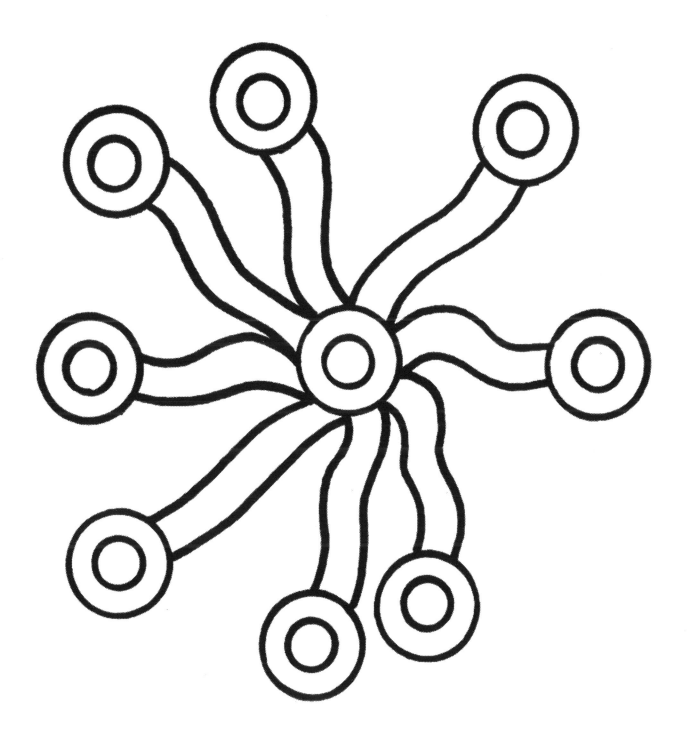

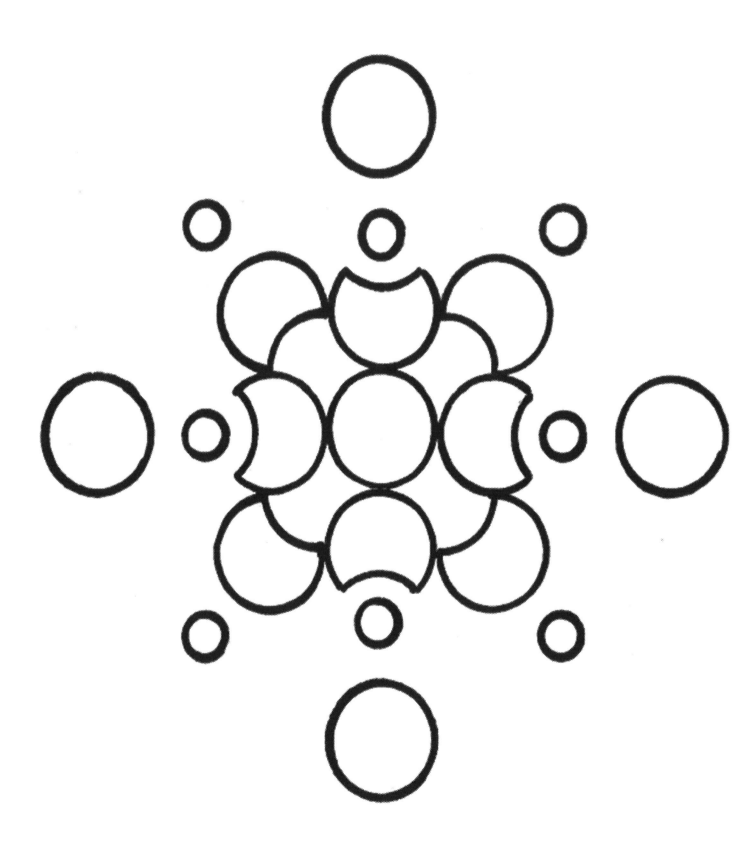

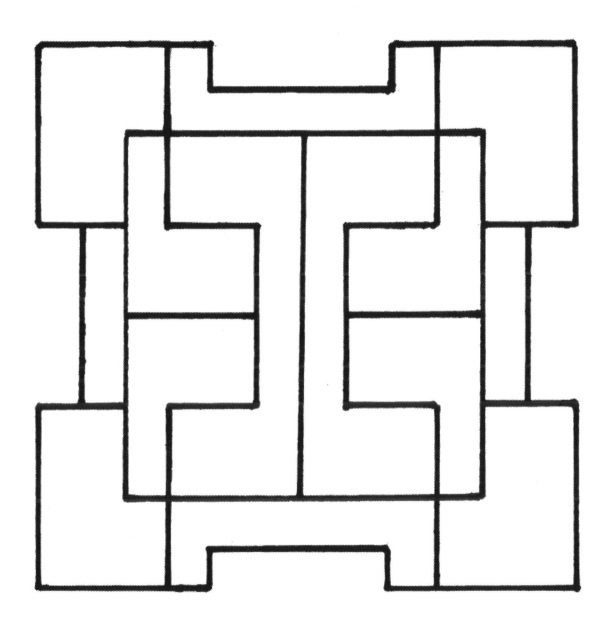

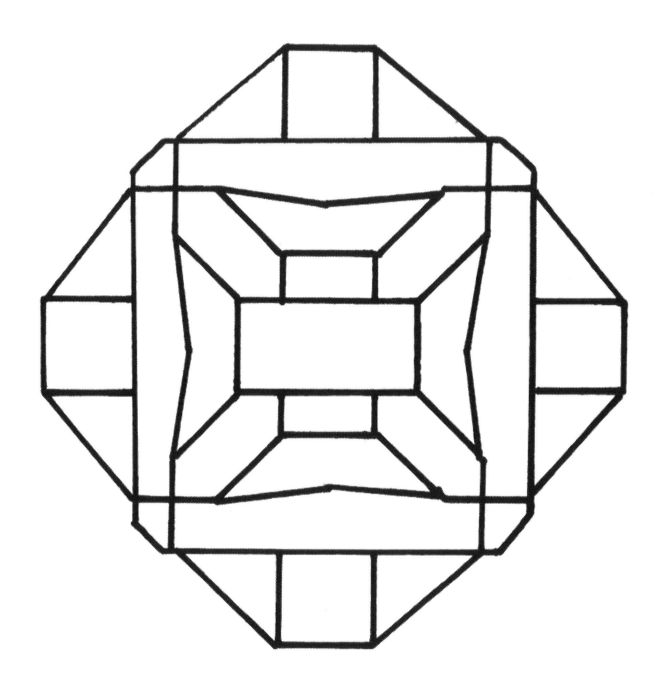

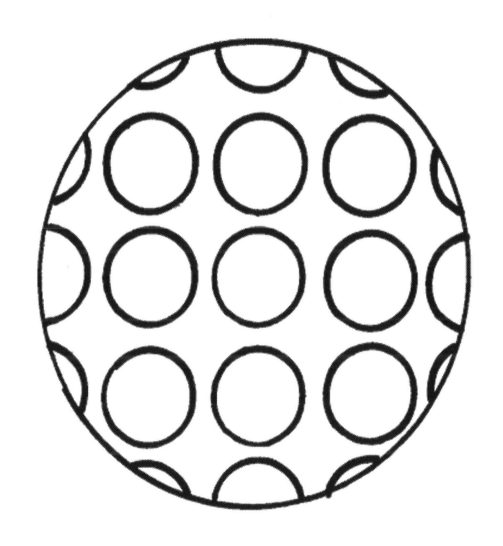

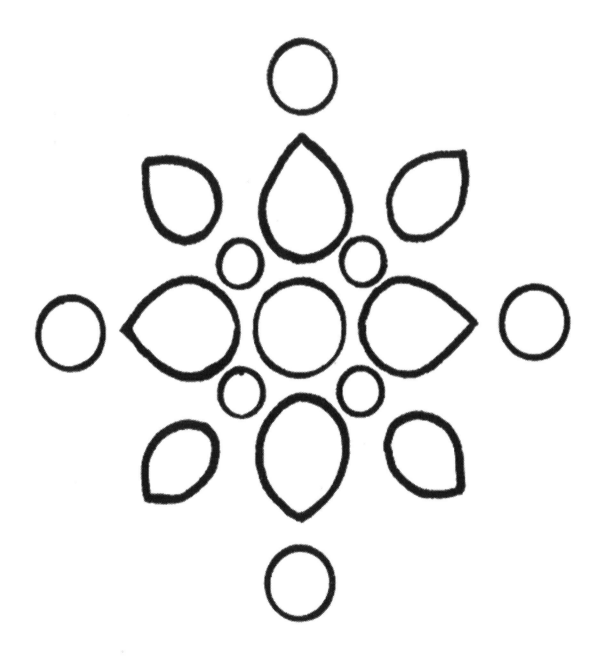

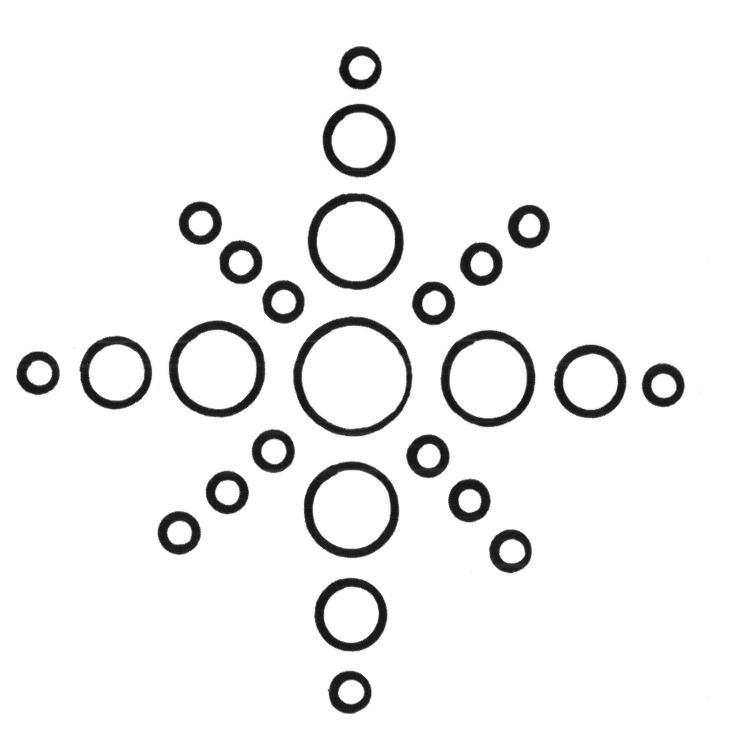

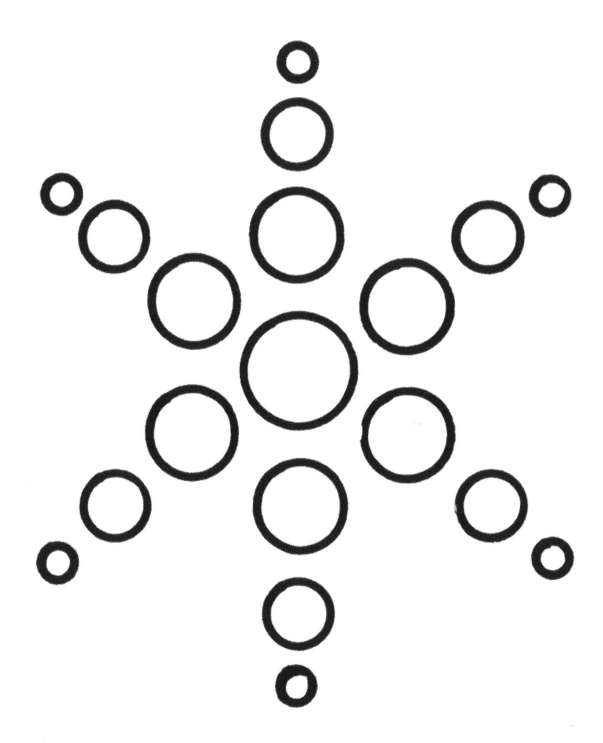

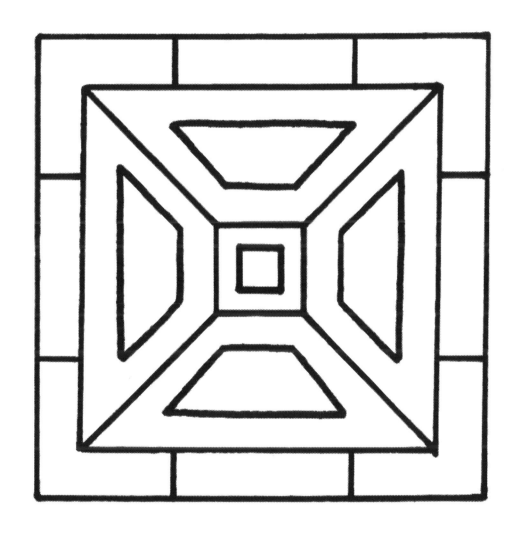

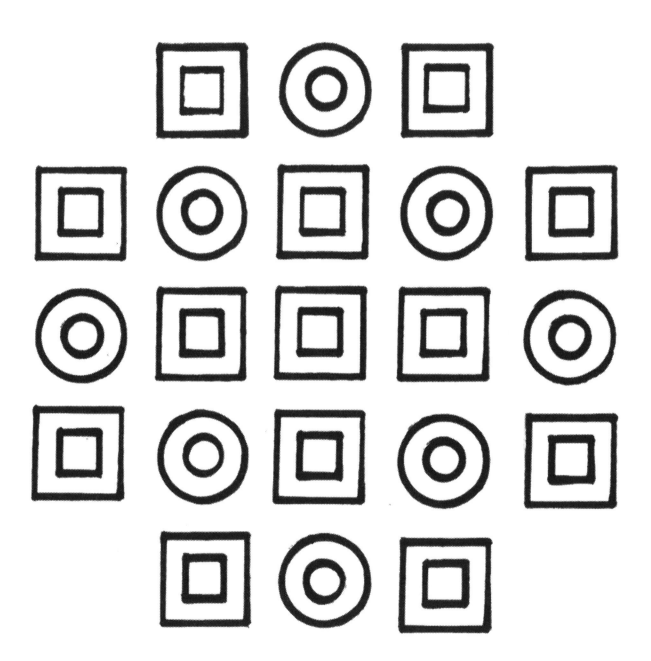

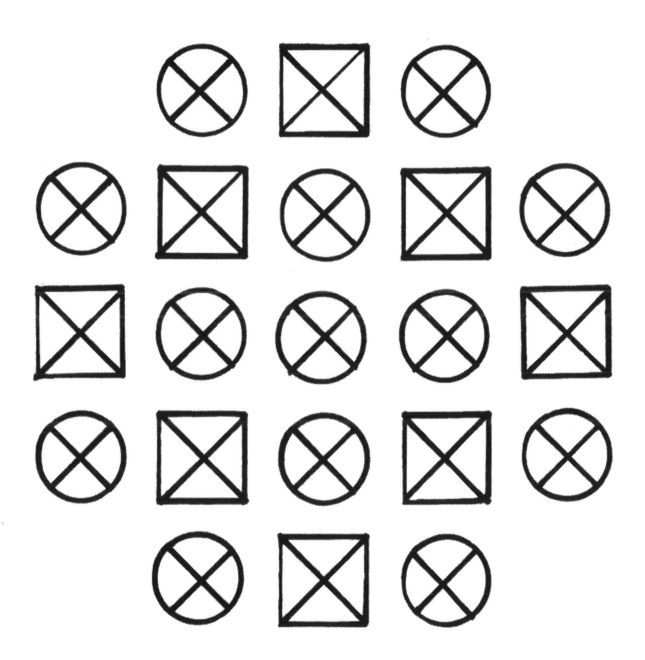

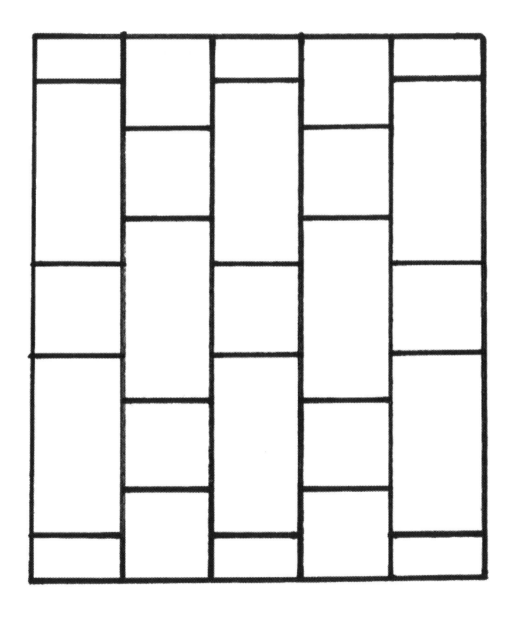

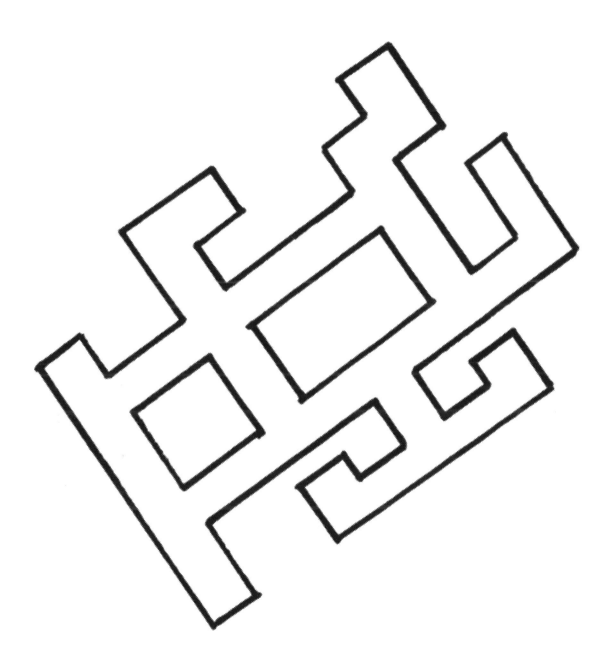

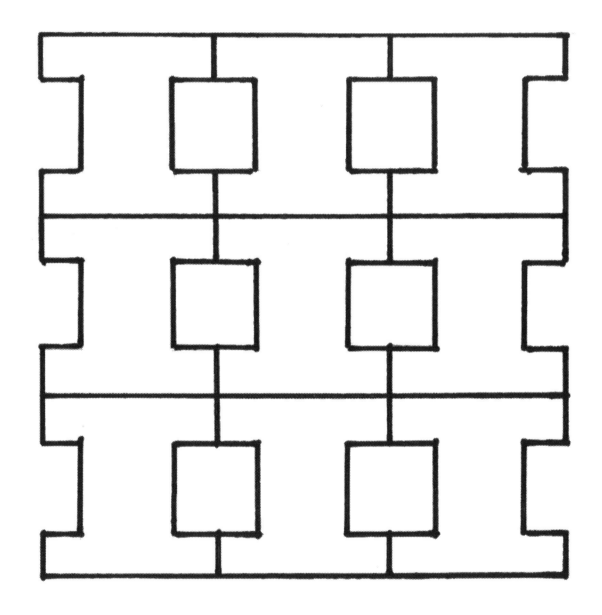

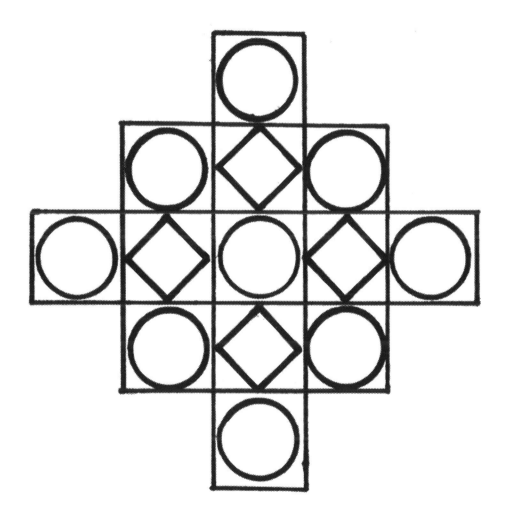

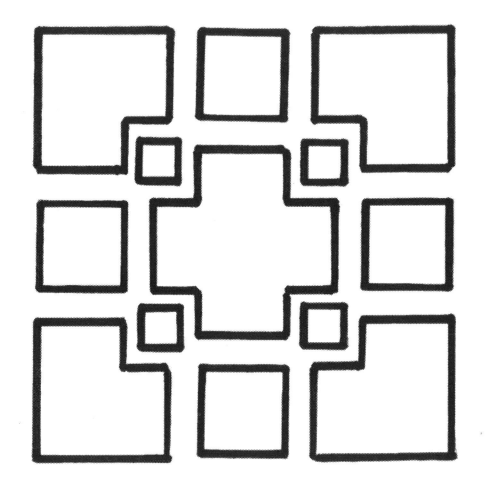

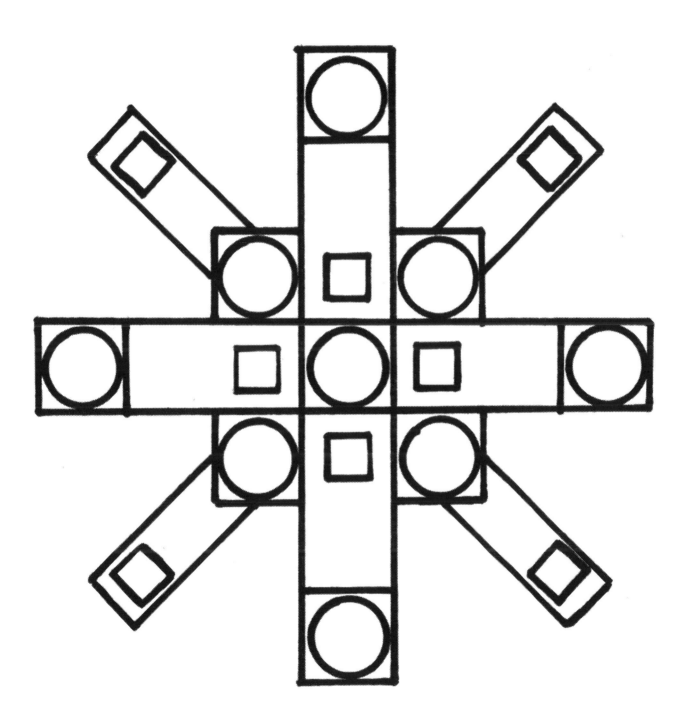

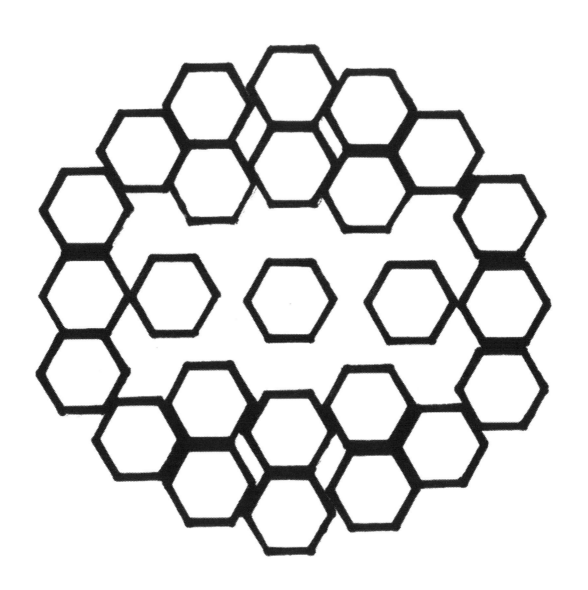

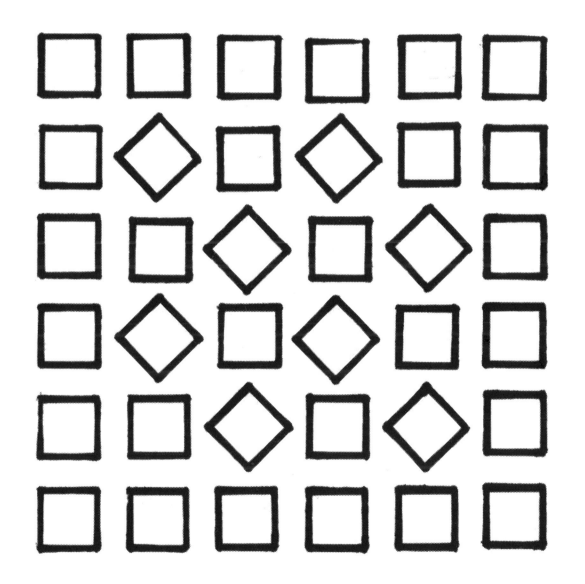

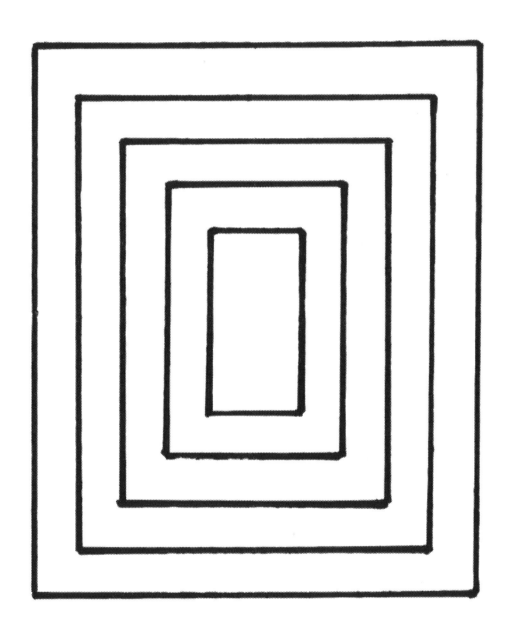

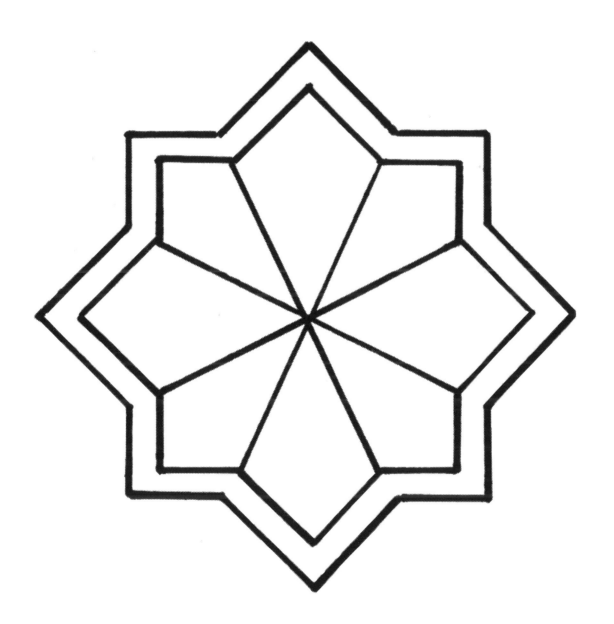

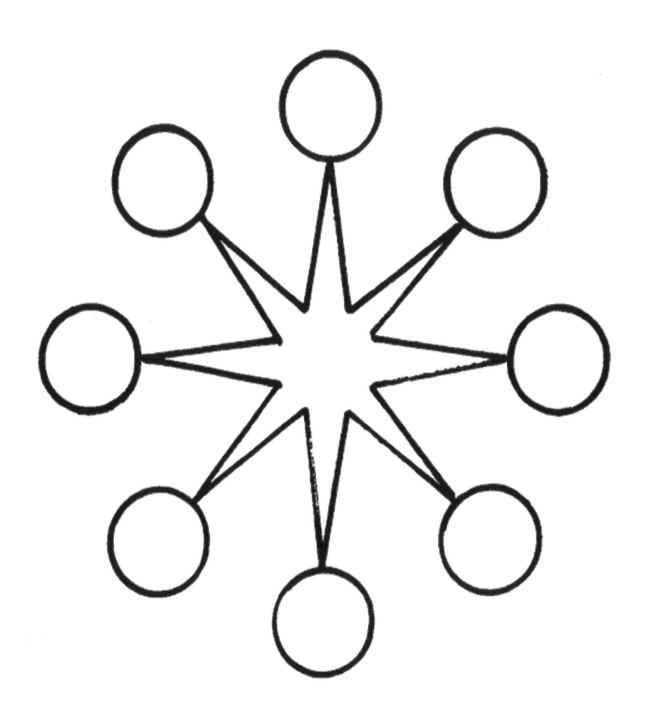

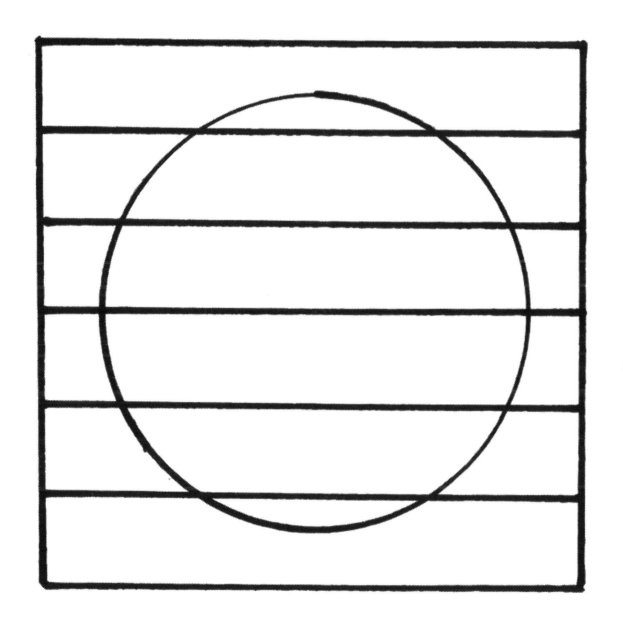

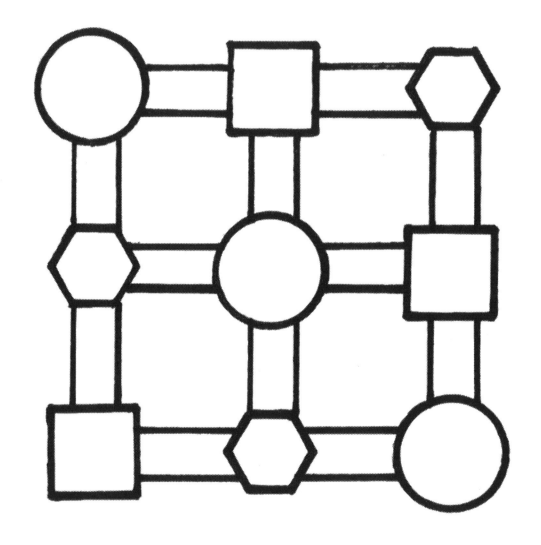

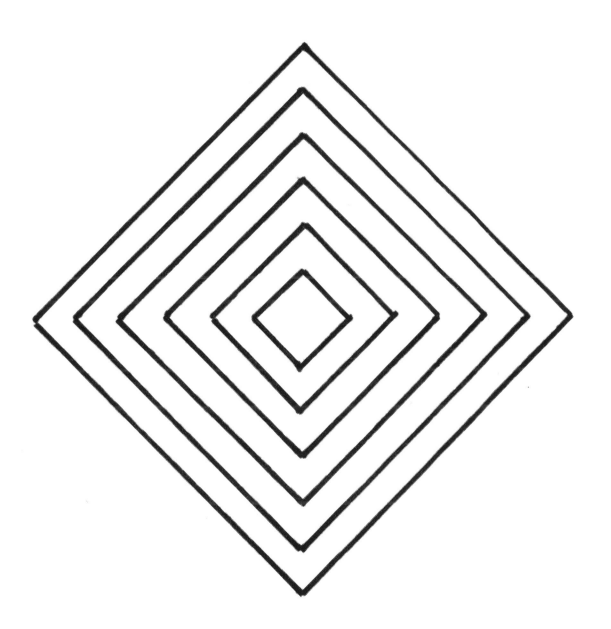

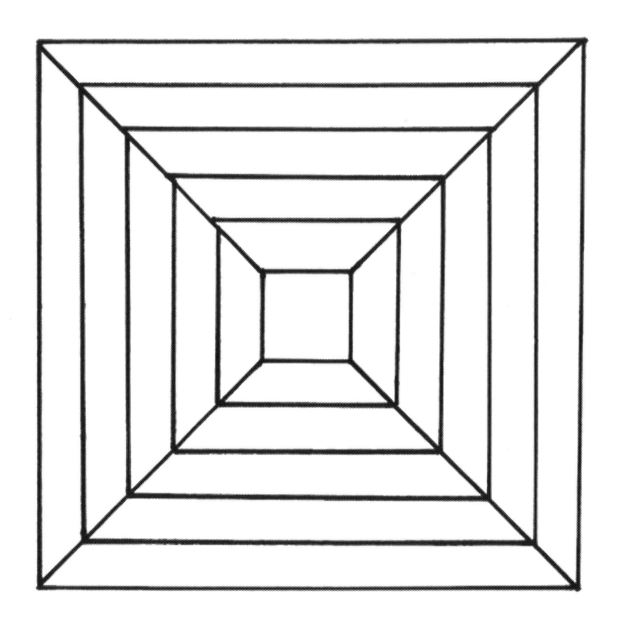

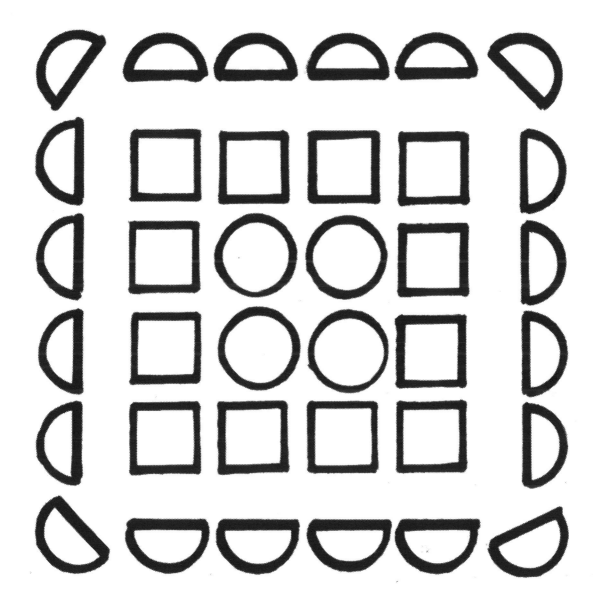

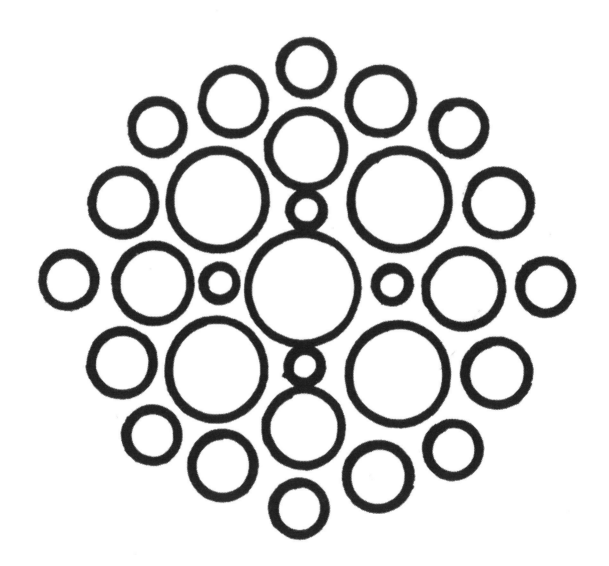

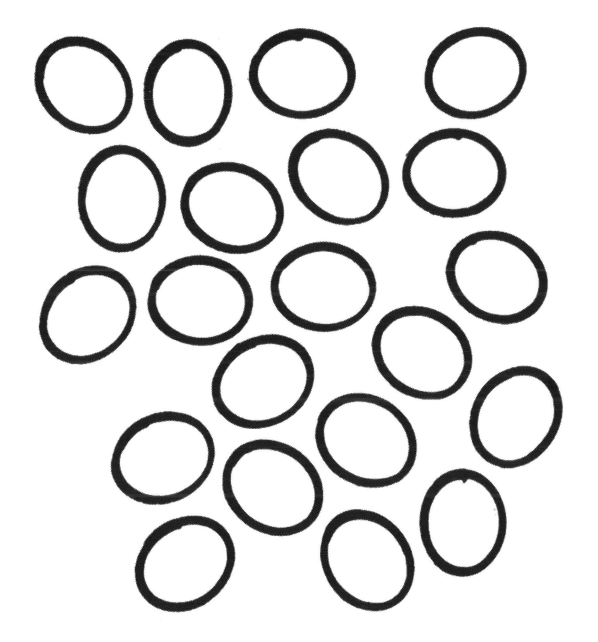

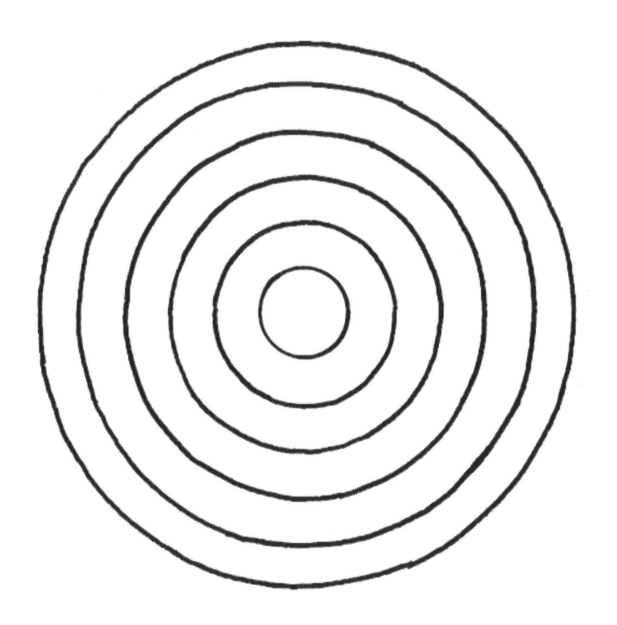

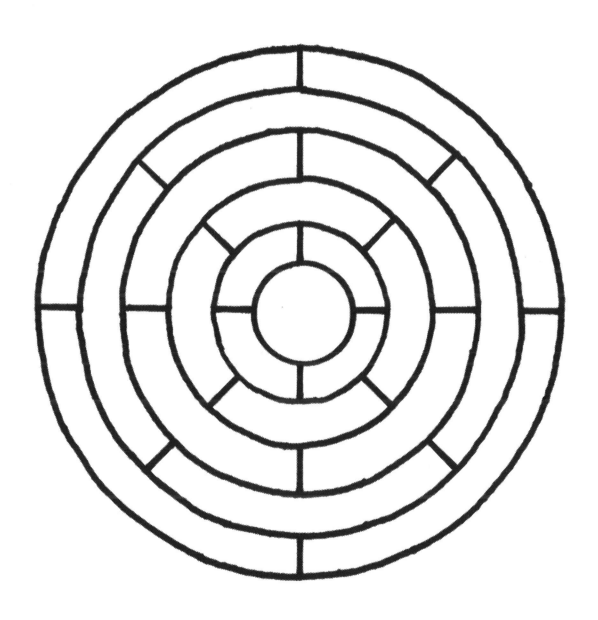

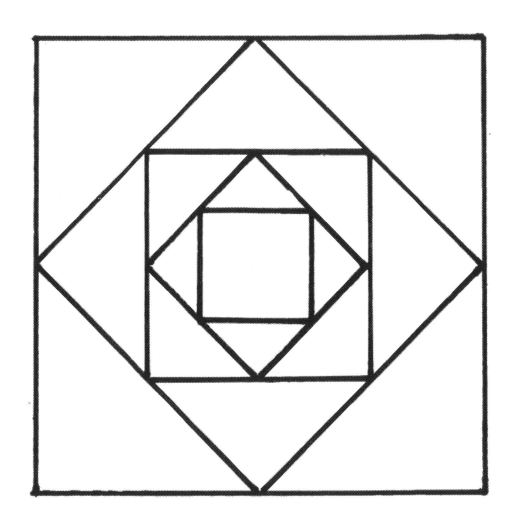

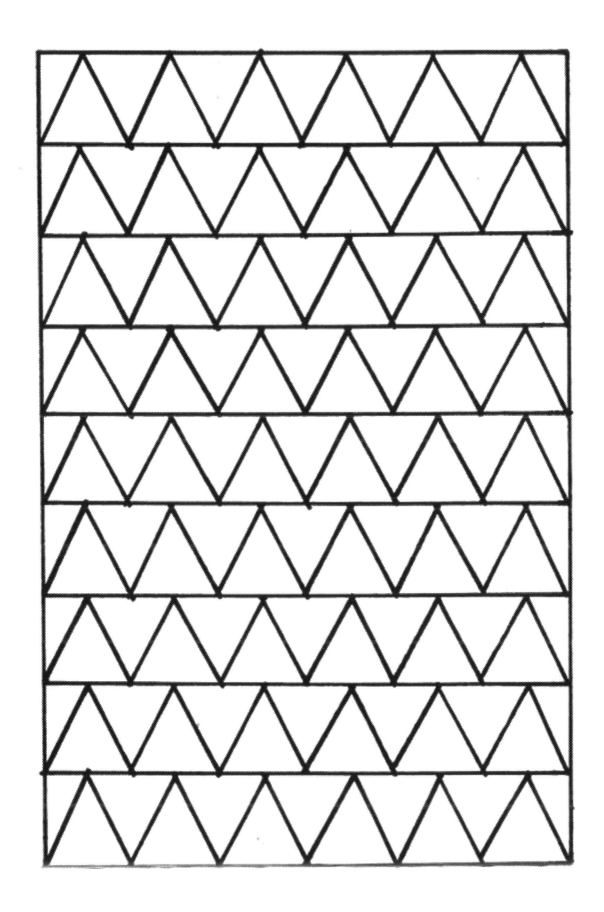

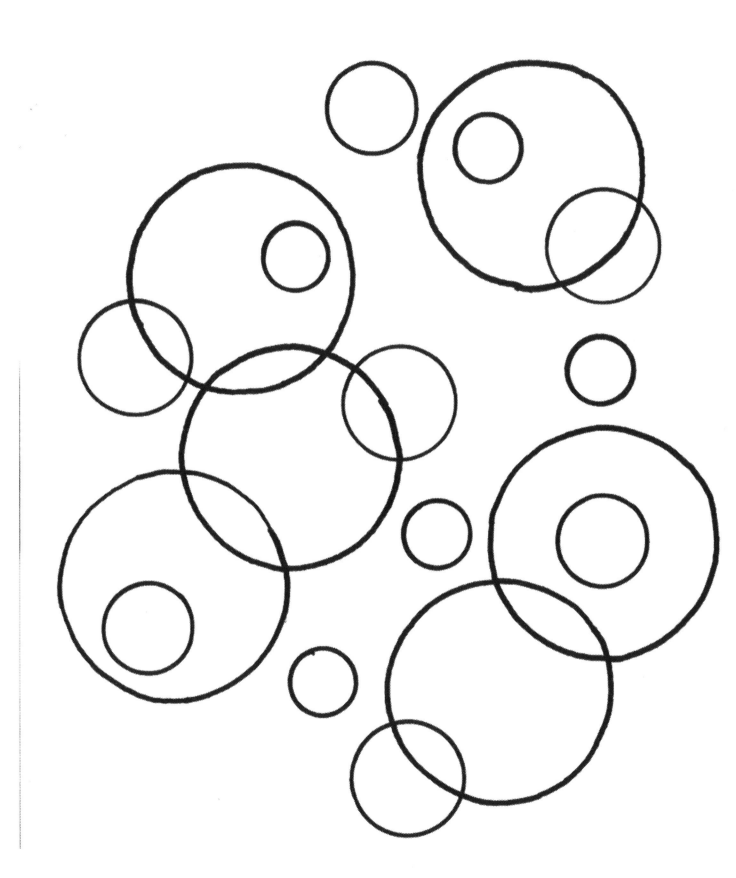

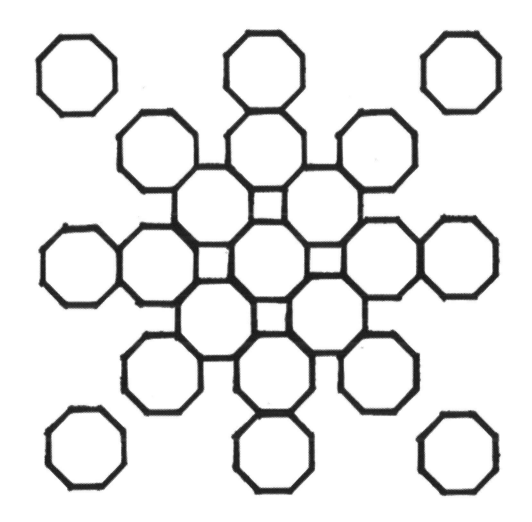

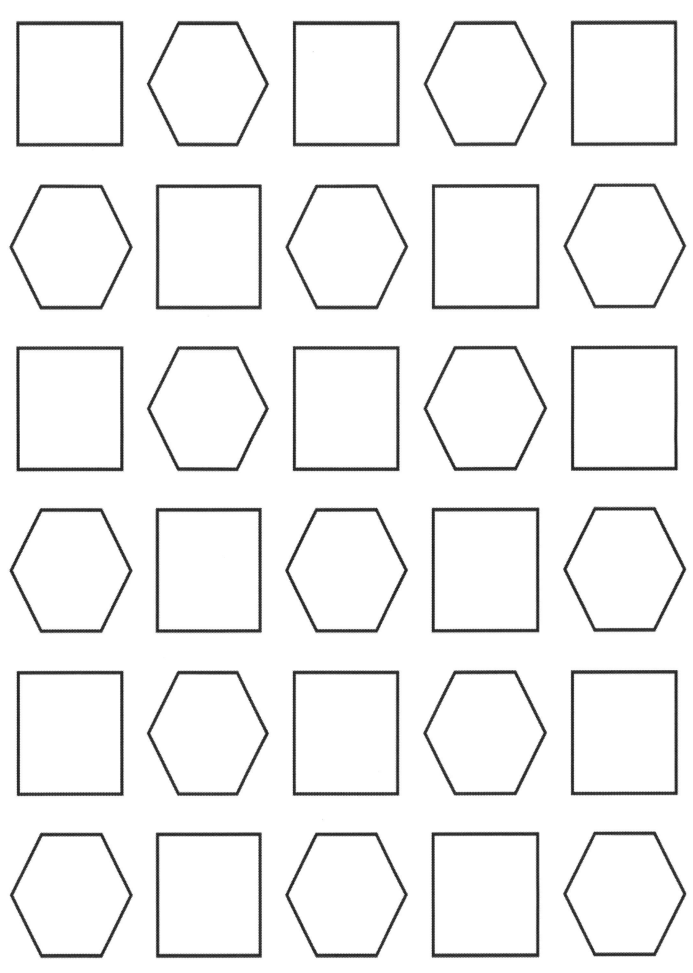

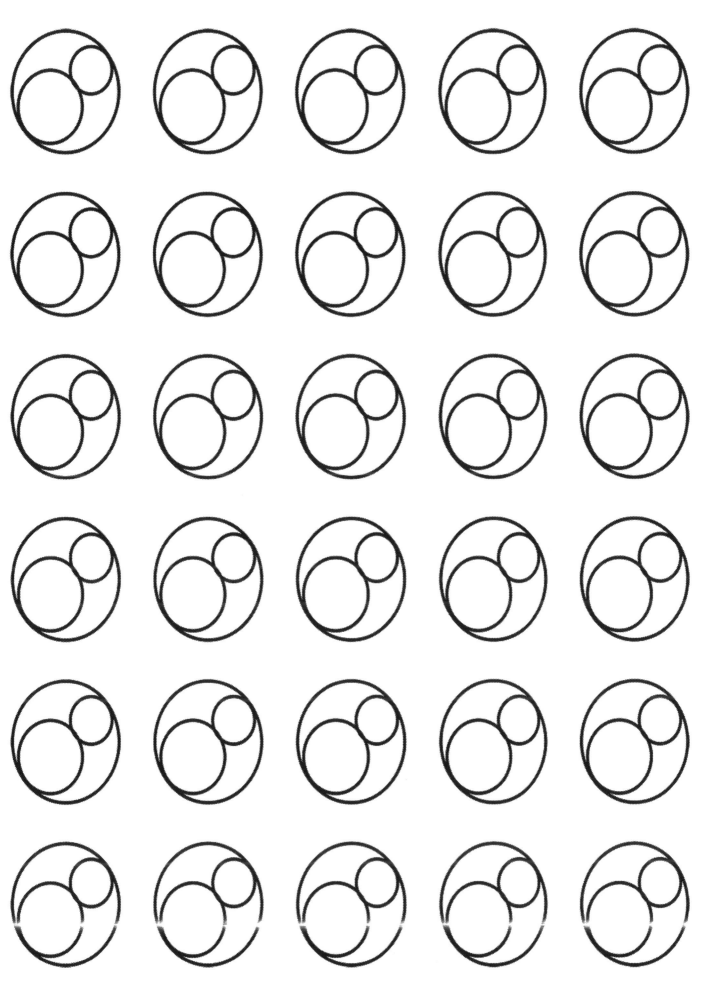

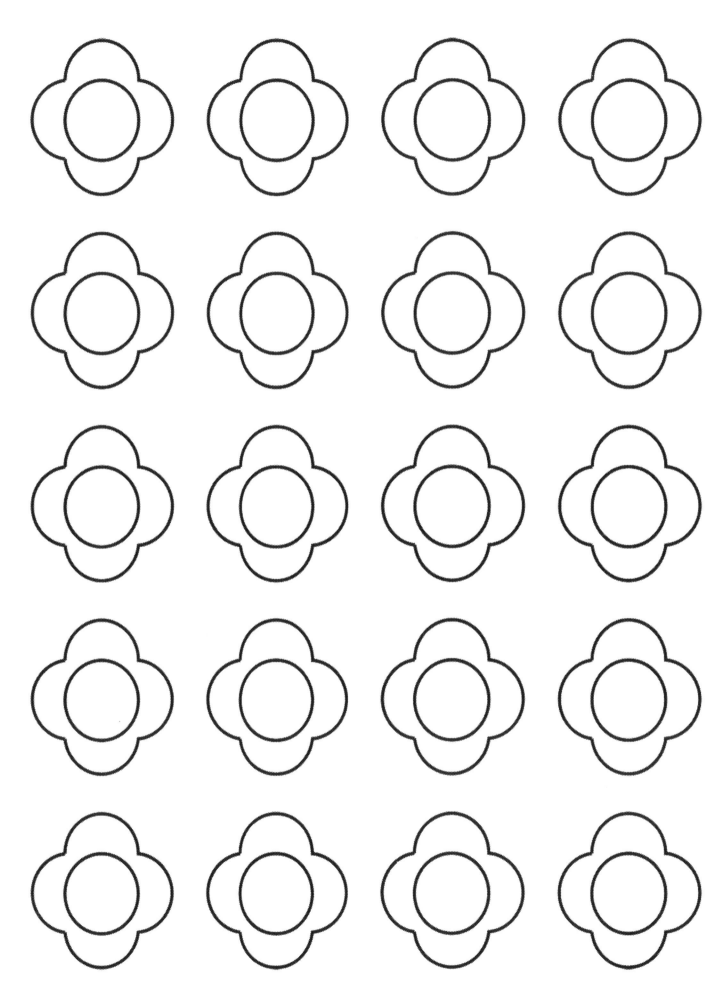

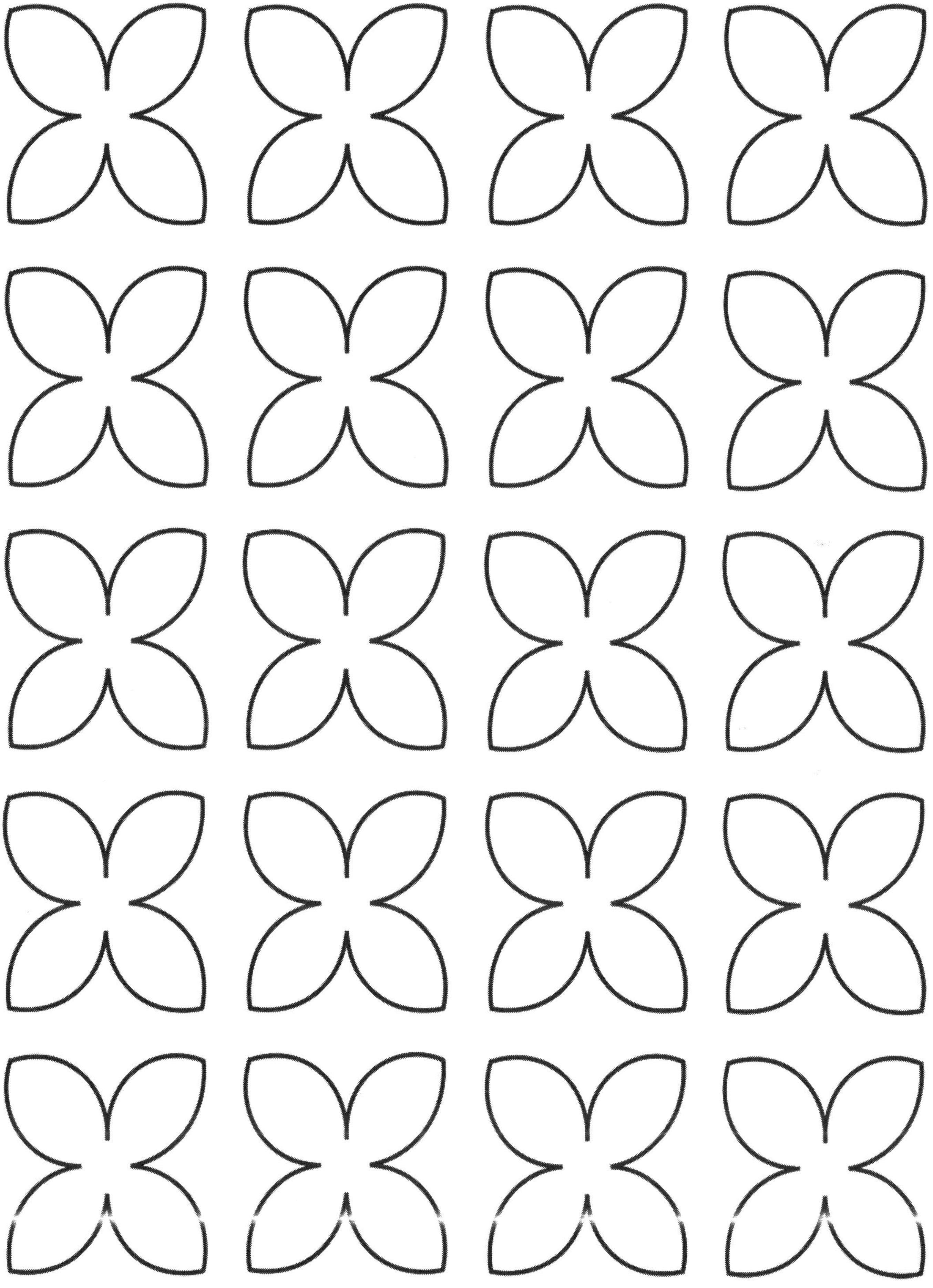

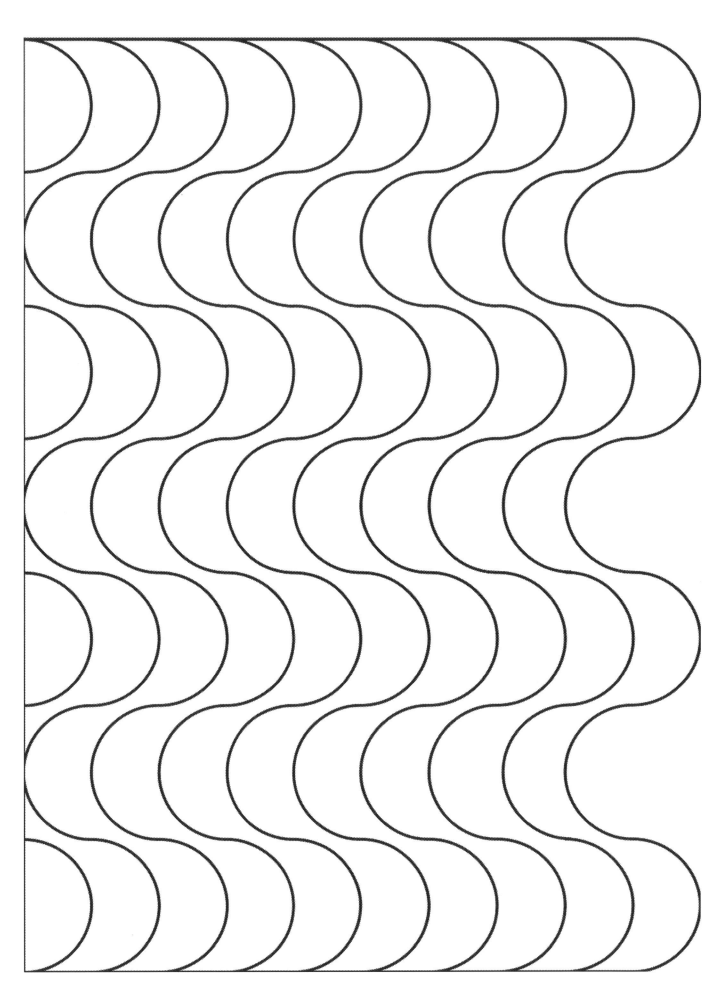

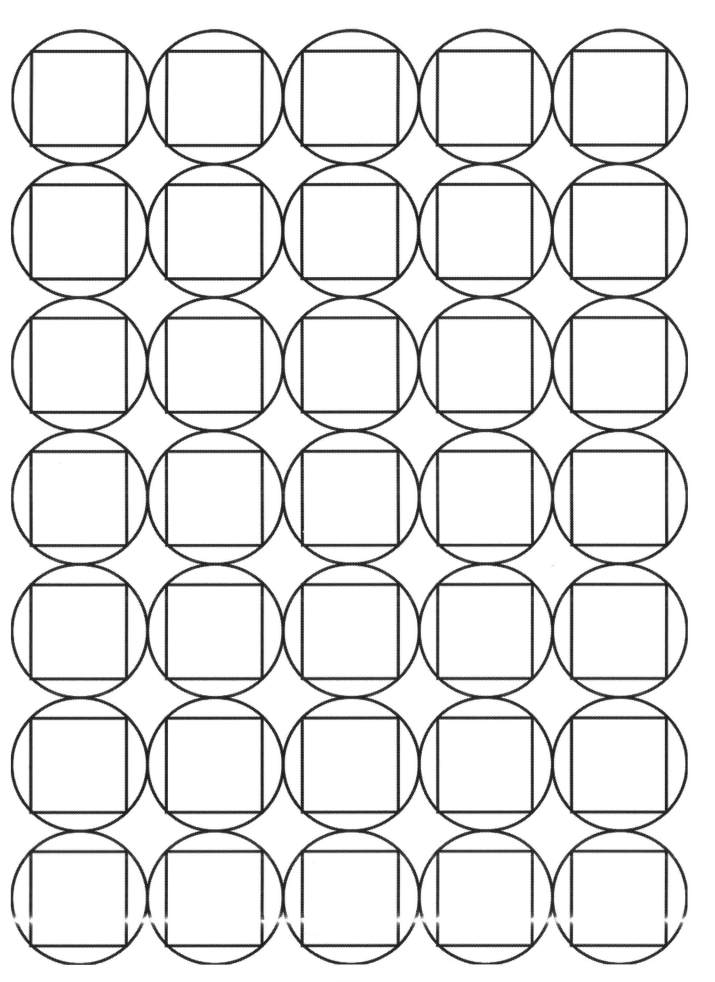

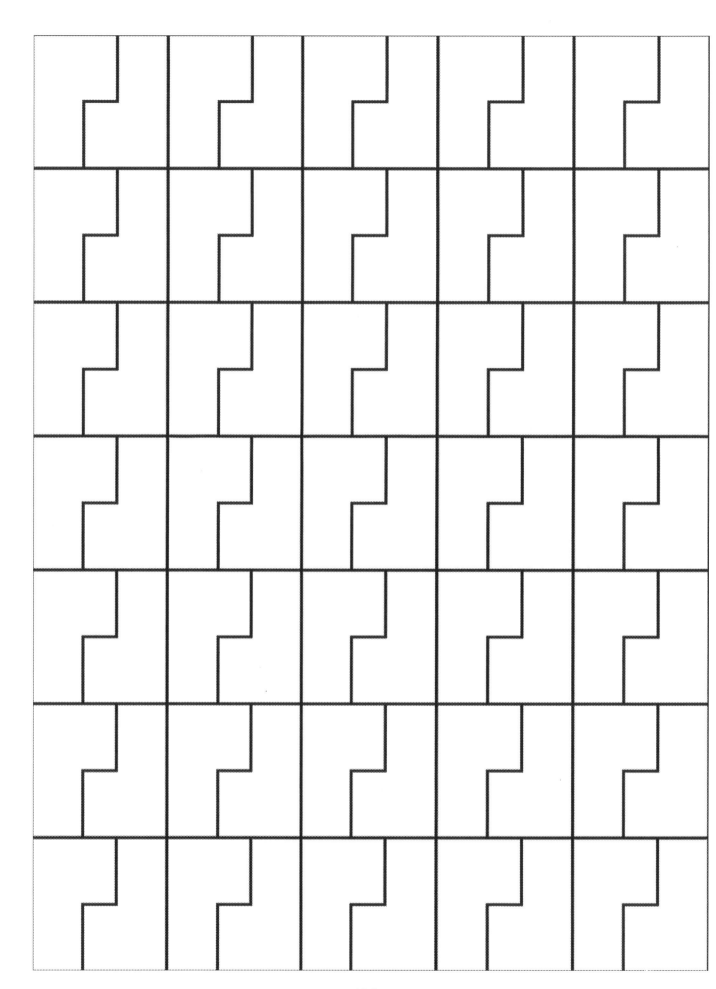

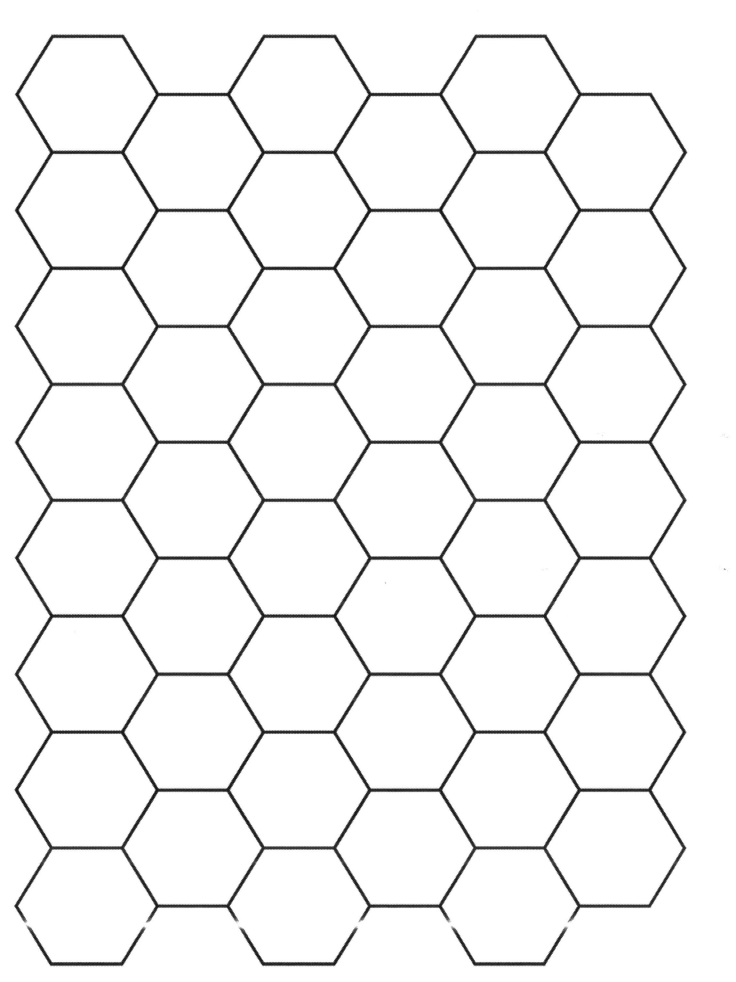

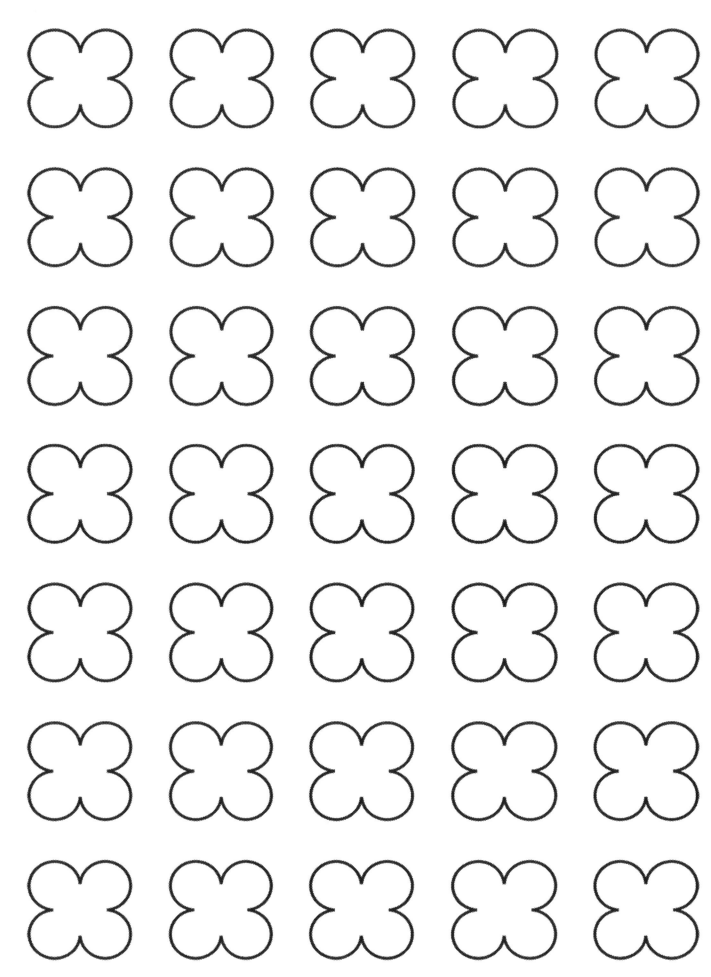

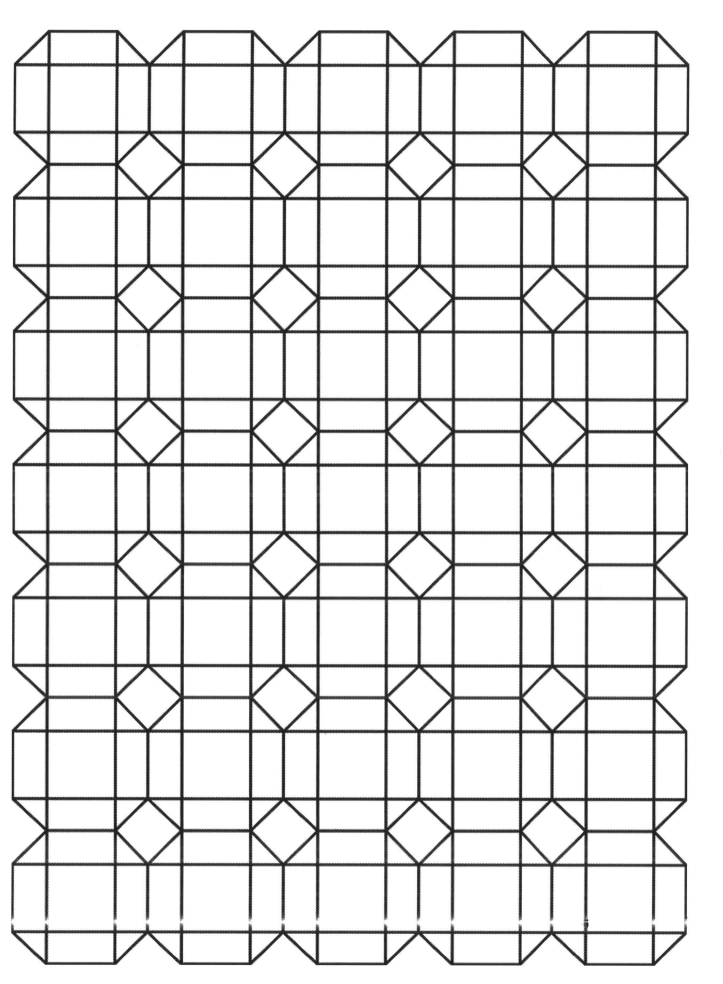

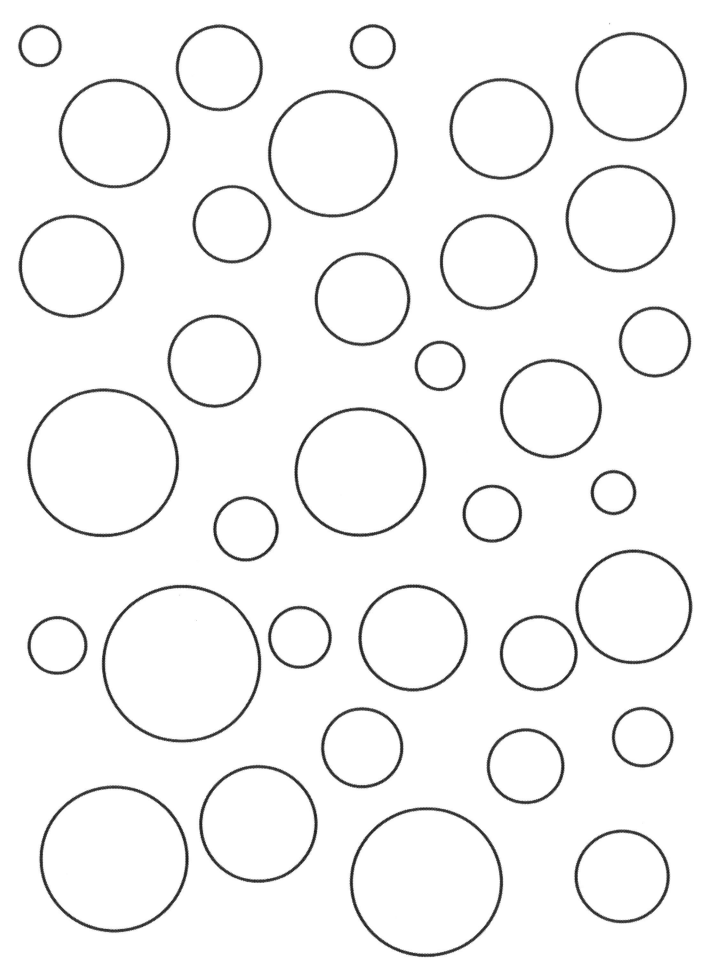

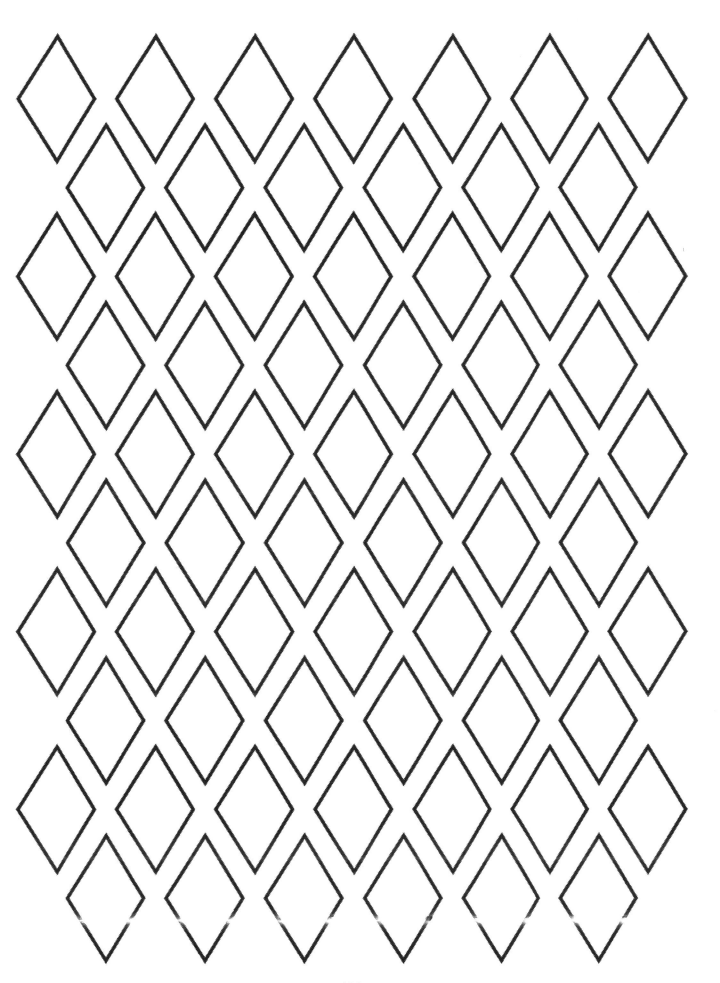

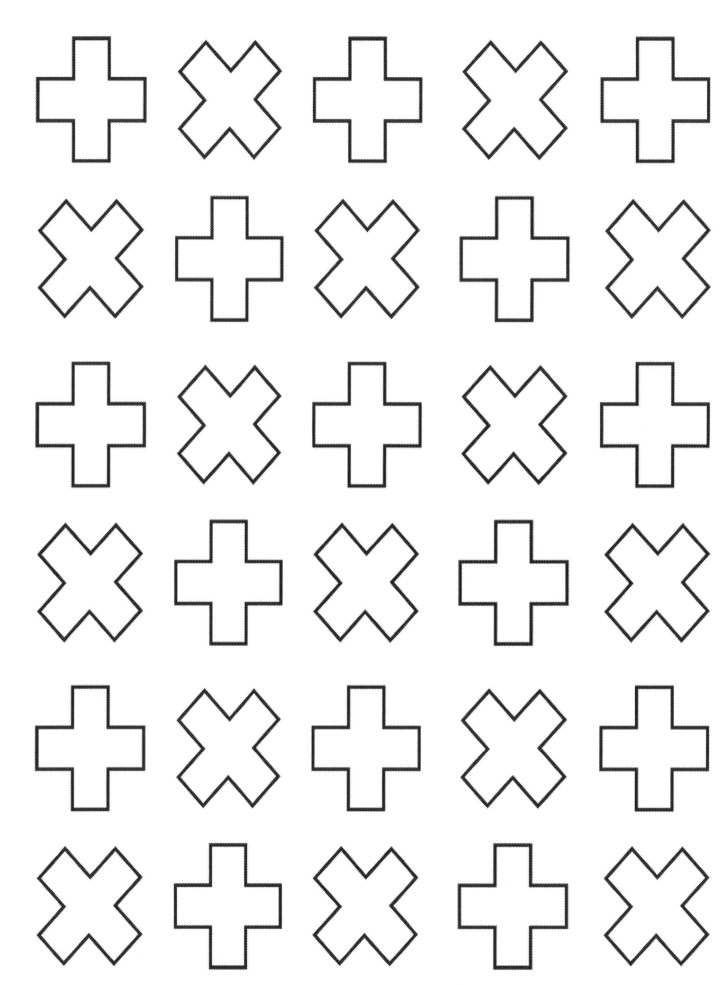

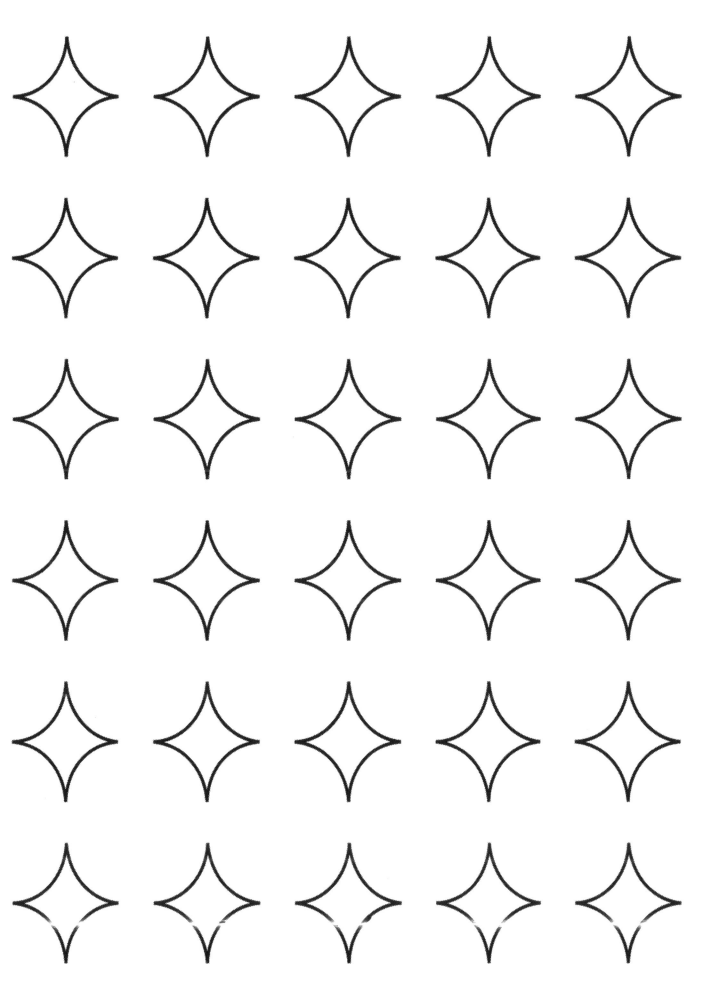

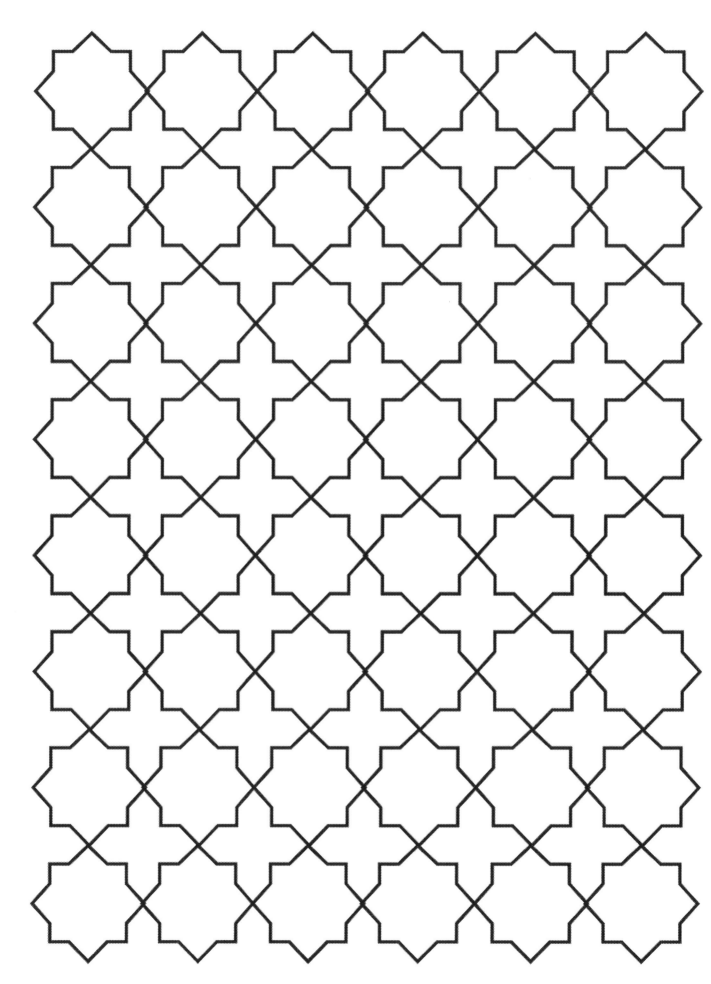

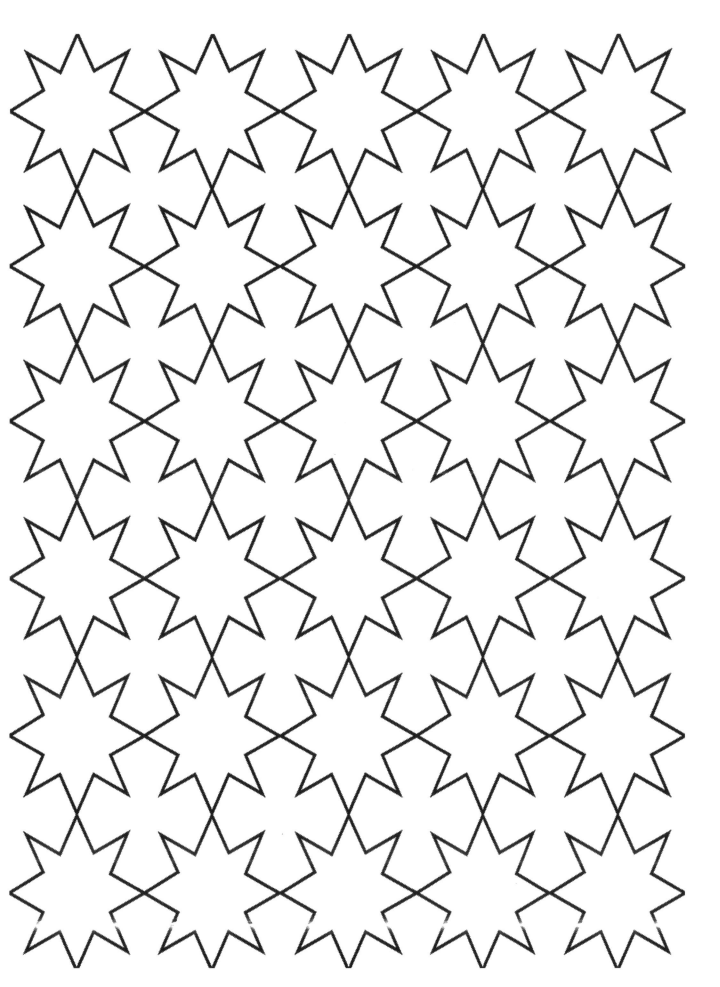

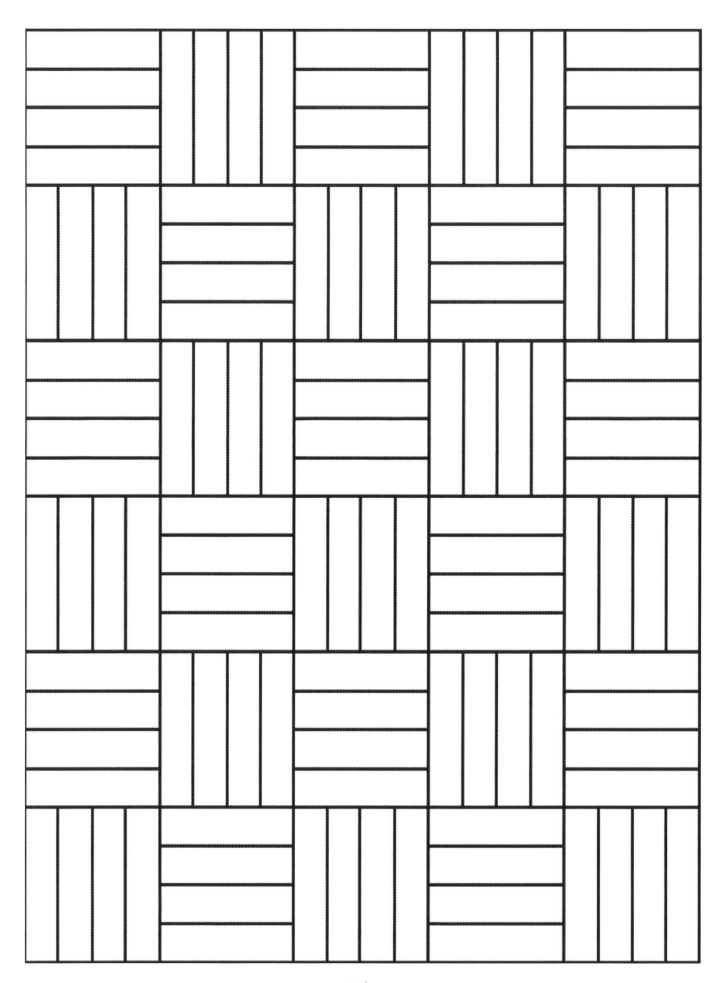

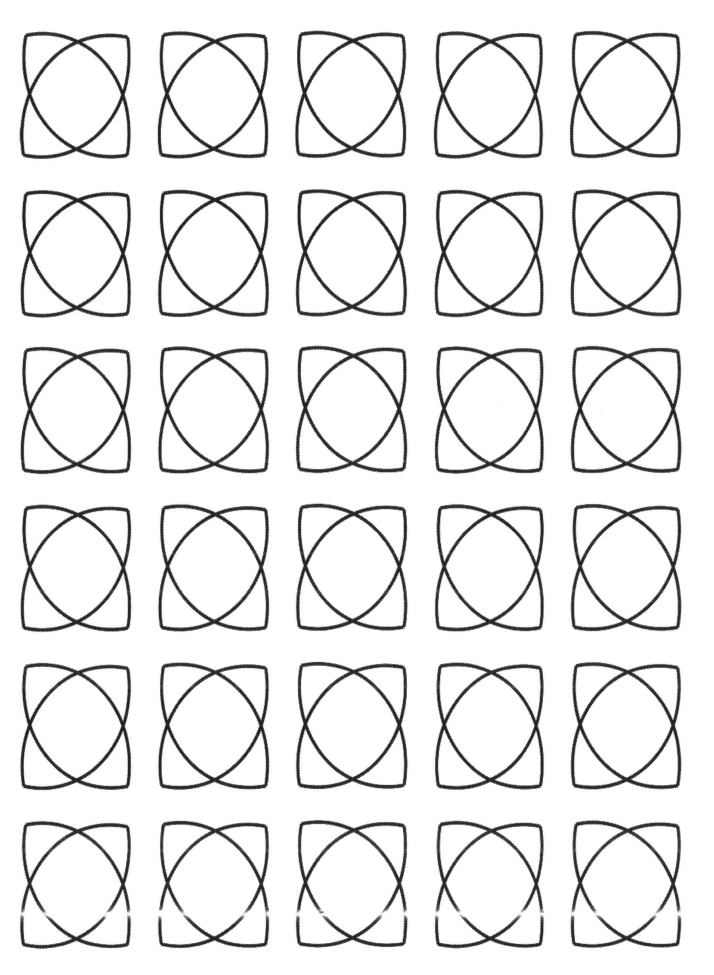

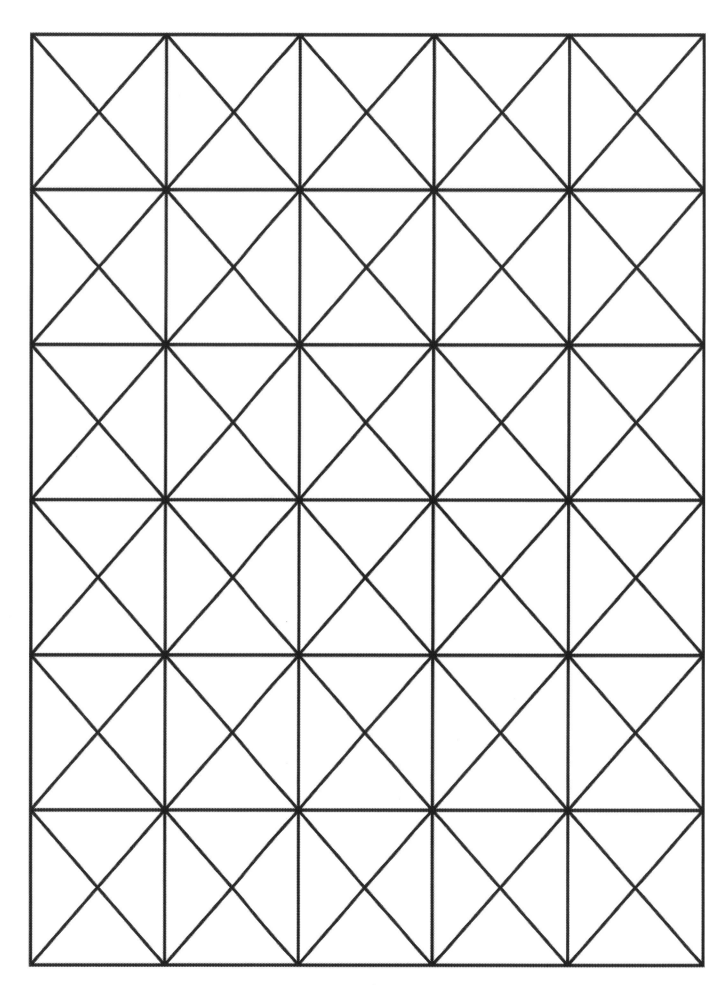

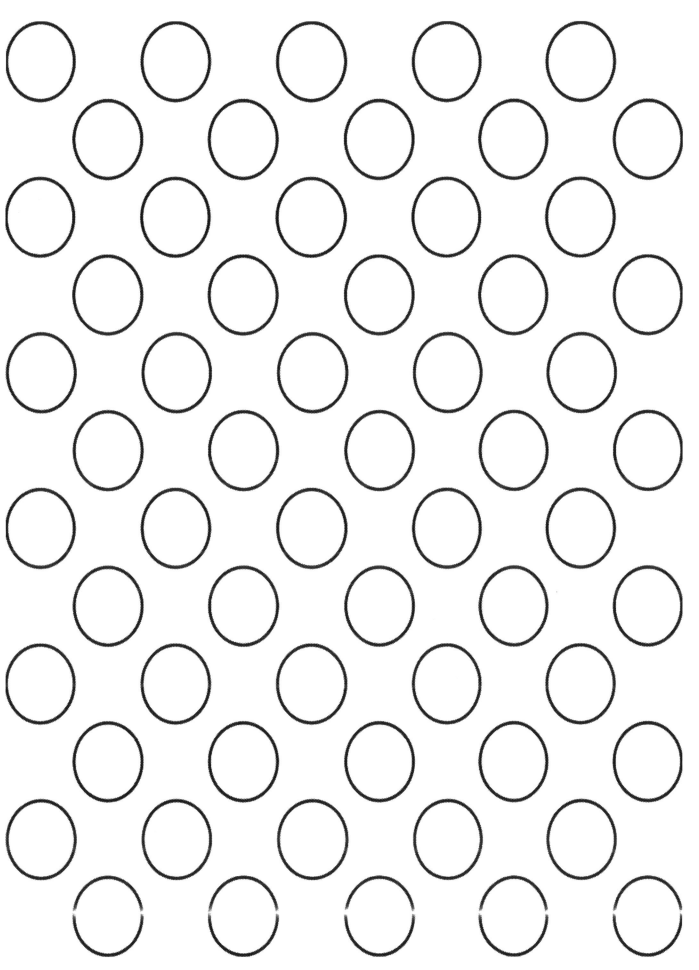

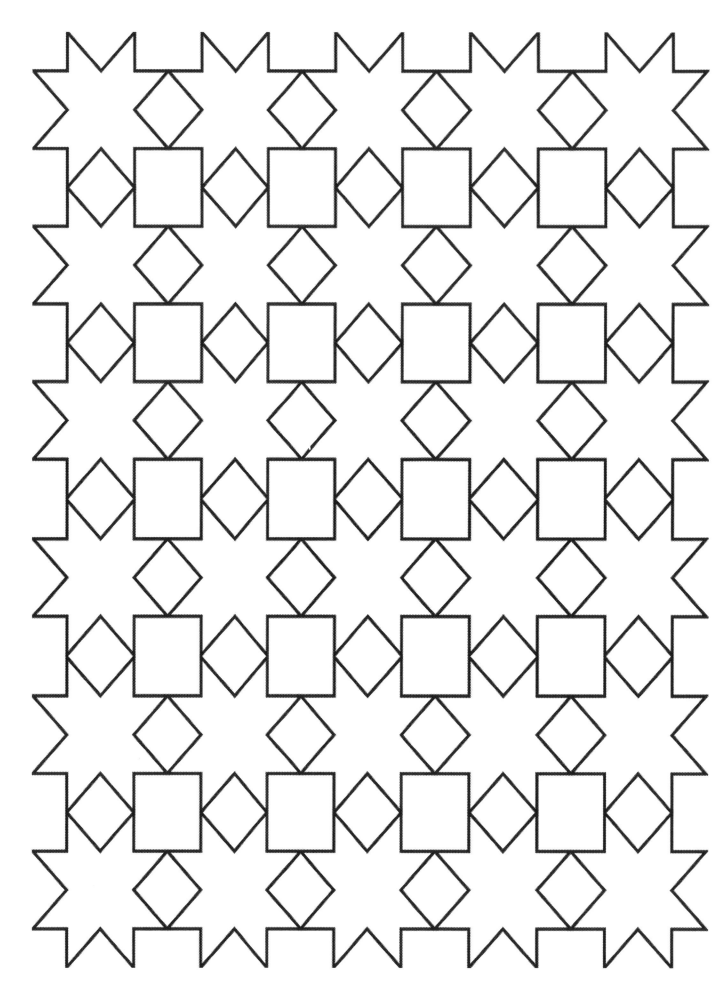

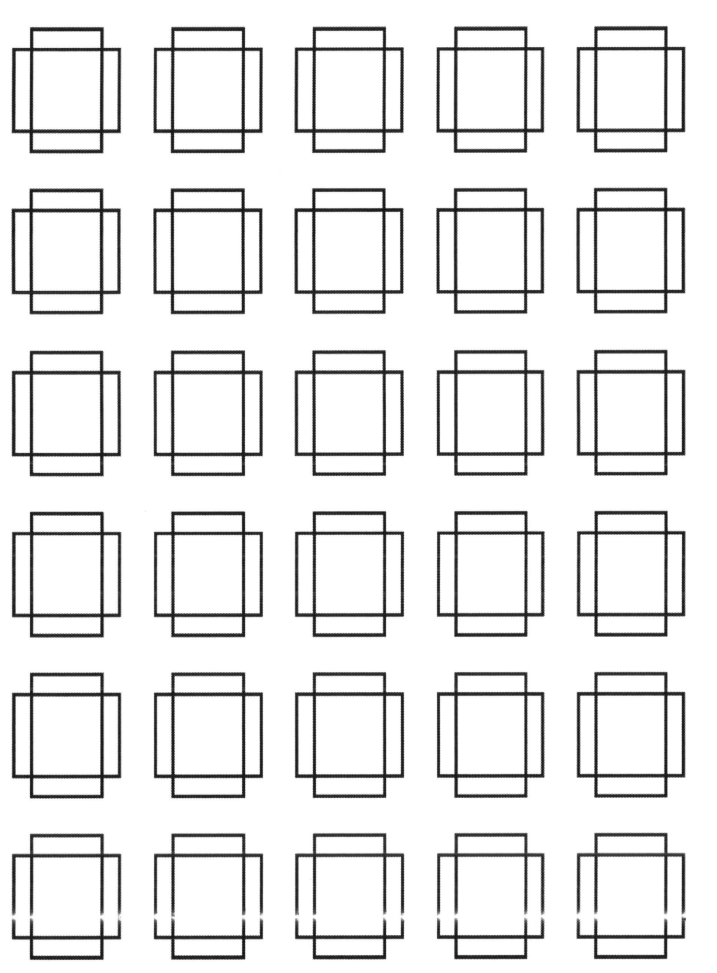

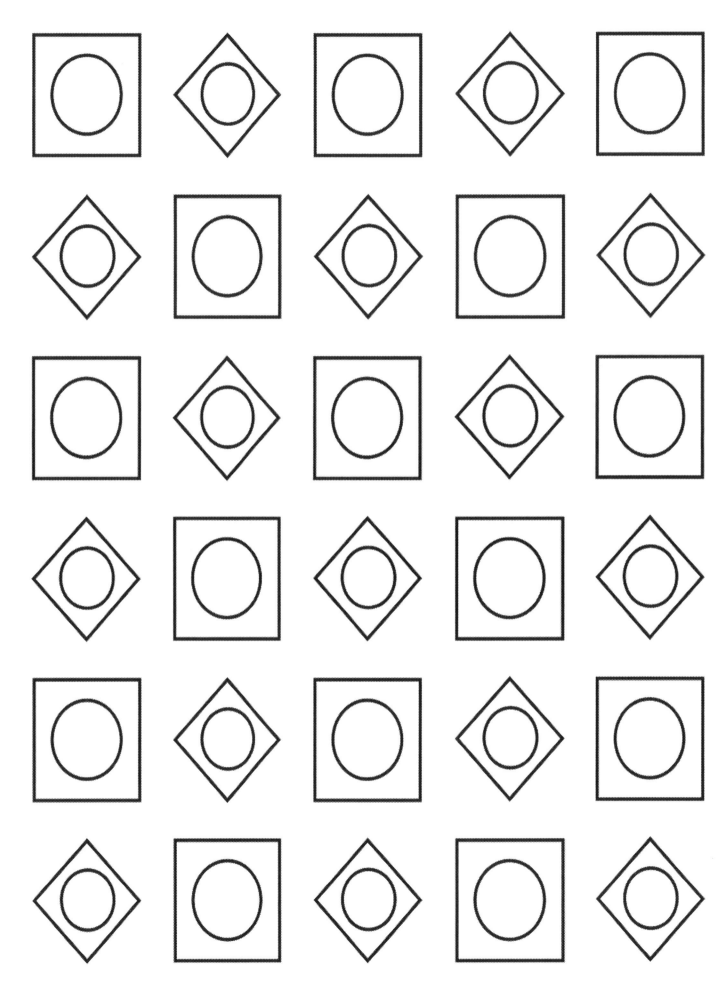

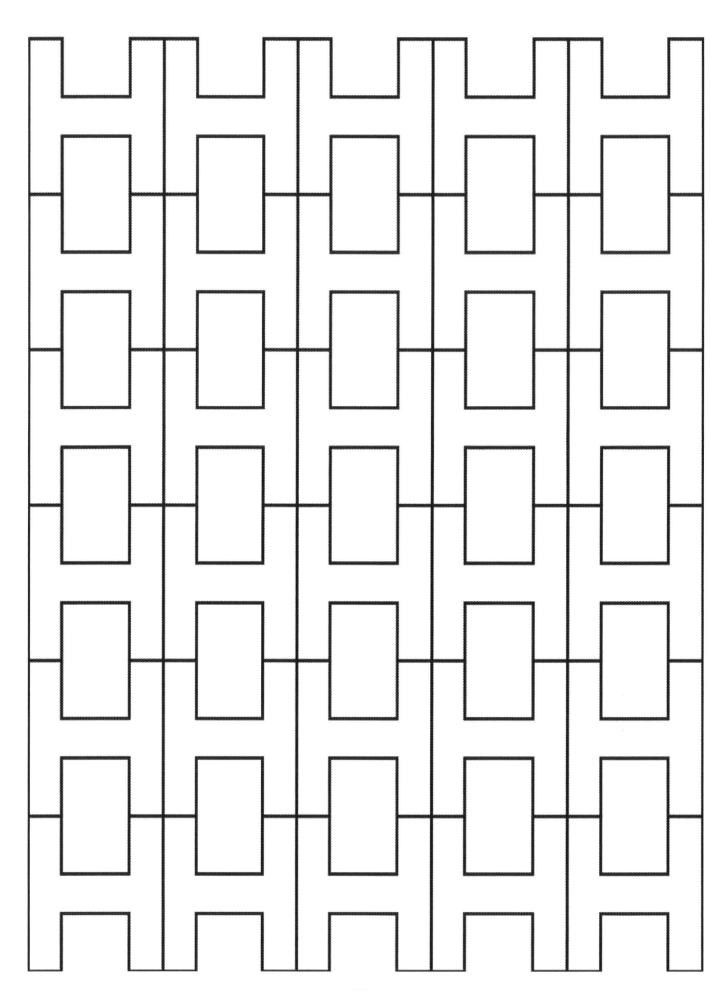

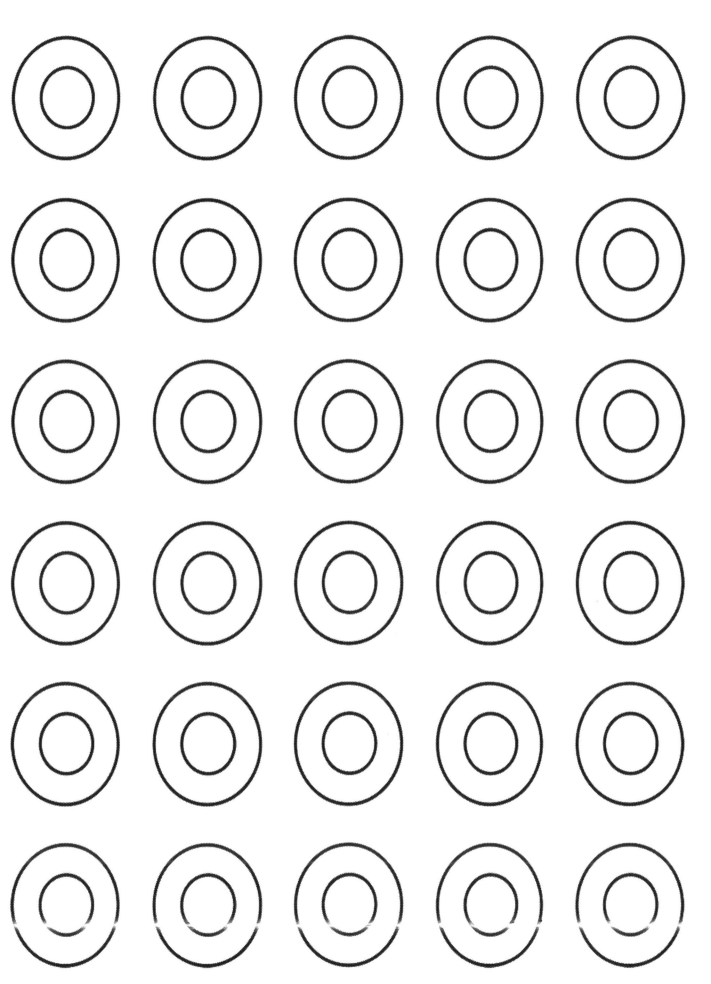

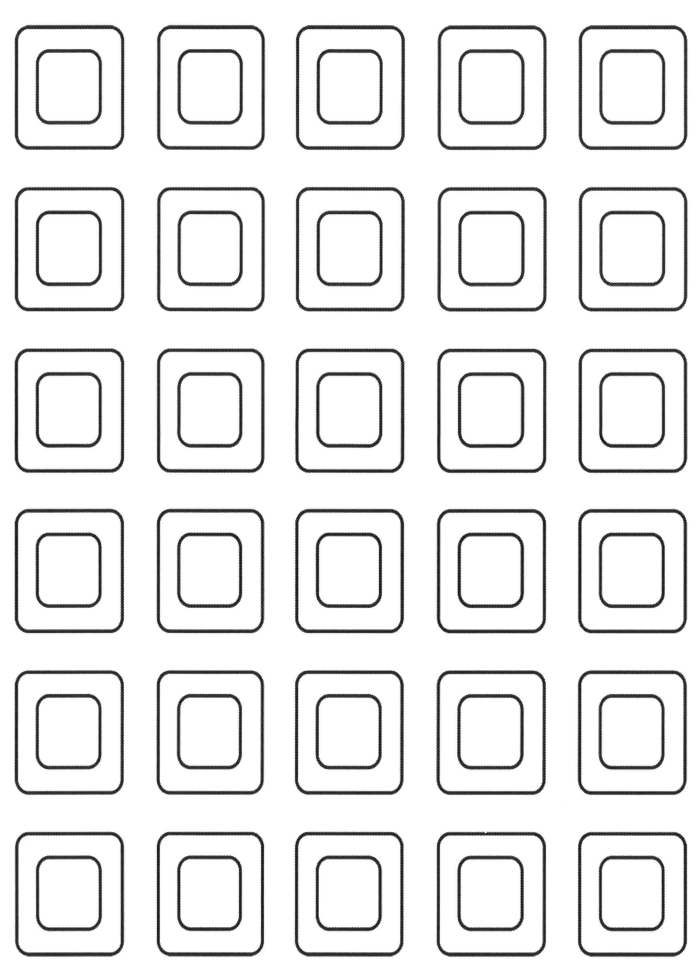

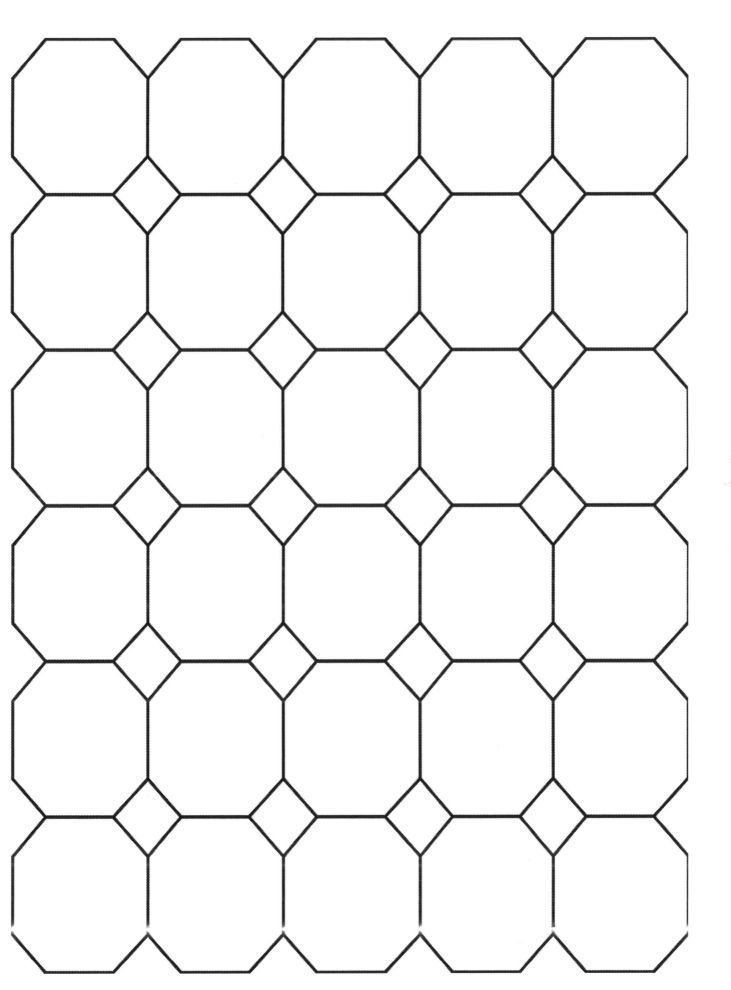

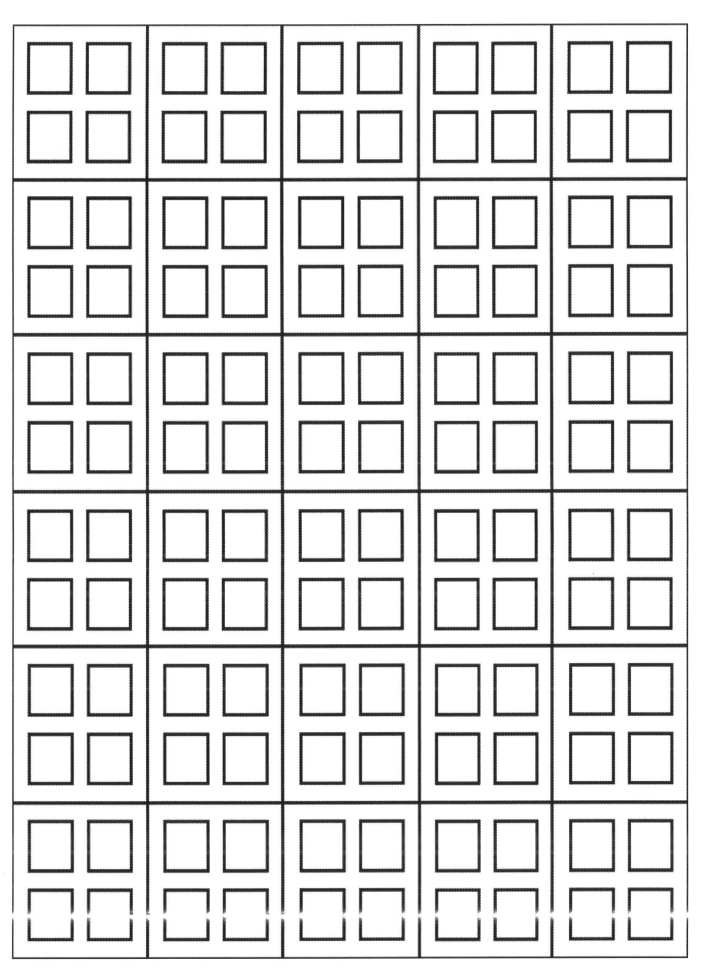

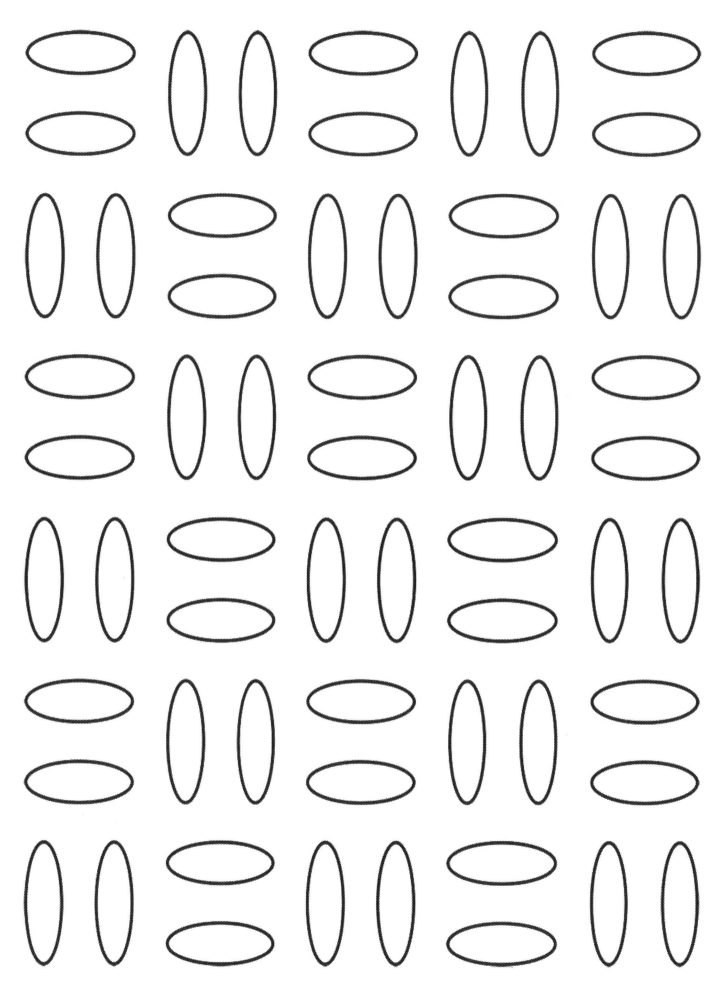

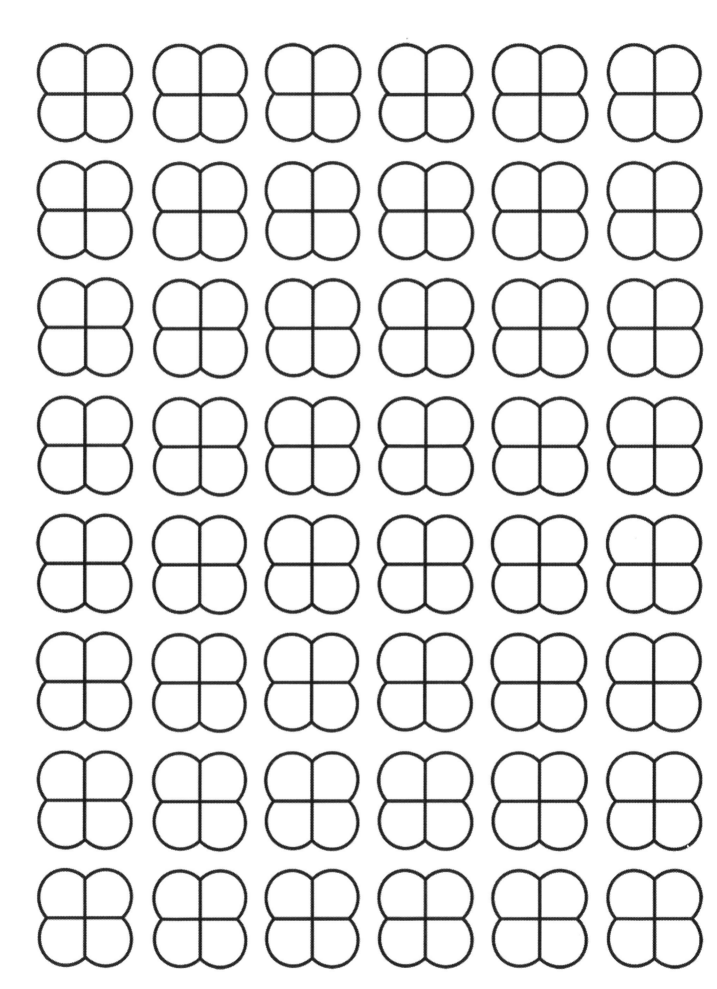

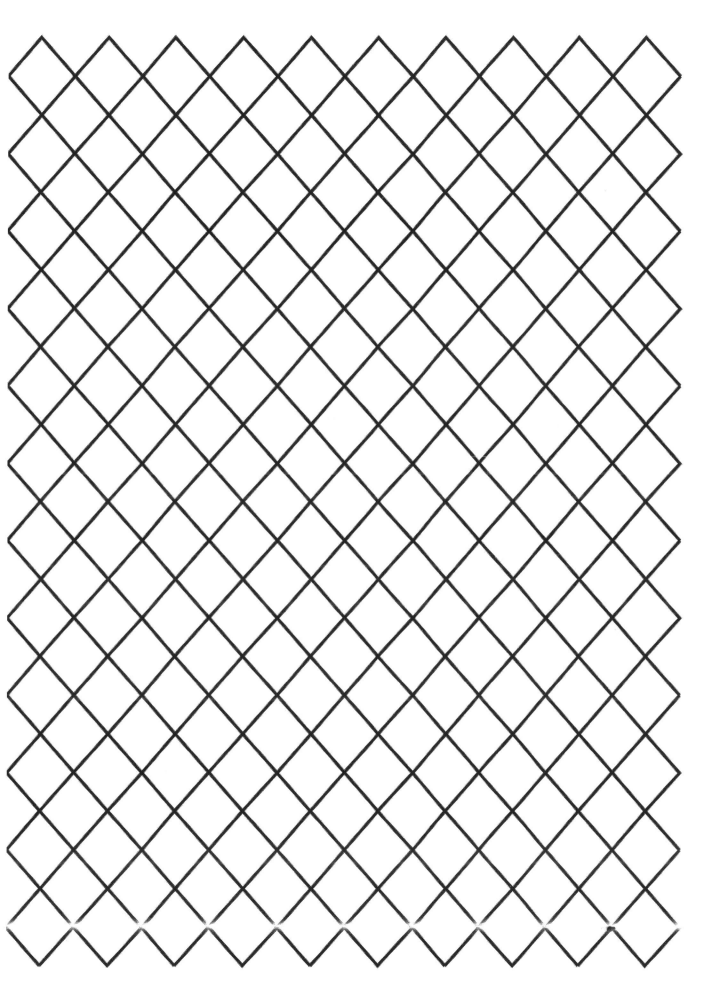